Ba 15
P

REVIVAL SERMONS

REVIVAL SERMONS

Evangelistic sermons
Preached through the years
In many revival meetings

By

PORTER M. BAILES
Pastor First Baptist Church
Tyler, Texas

BROADMAN PRESS
NASHVILLE, TENNESSEE

1000—8-38—4

Printed in the United States of America

DEDICATED TO
MY WIFE
SARAH BUTTON BAILES
MOTHER OF OUR TWO BOYS
PORTER, JR., AND JOE DEAN
WHOSE
SENSITIVE SPIRIT
CULTURED SOUL
CONSECRATED LIFE
AND
LOYAL DEVOTION

HAVE BEEN A CONSTANT SOURCE OF INSPIRATION AND A
COMPELLING FORCE IN MY LIFE AS A MINISTER

(5)

FOREWORD

Great is the responsibility of one who essays the task of writing even a brief introduction to a book of any nature. This responsibility is heightened when the publication is to consist of a volume of sermons.

Dr. Porter M. Bailes, pastor of the First Baptist Church of Tyler, Texas, delivered many of the sermons in this book during our annual revival at Baylor University, in October, 1937, to the great delight and profit of both our faculty and our student body.

Having heard these sermons, the memory of their uplifting power will linger with us for many years. Doctor Bailes preached with great power and earnestness to our students. He has combined in one person the qualities of an able pulpit orator, a clear and pointed interpreter of the gospel message as found in the Book of books, and a popular and helpful speaker to college young people as well as to the public generally. Indeed, he combines in a very fine and wholesome way keen spiritual insight, popular appeal, and moral earnestness.

Religious and civic leaders will welcome with delight this interesting volume of informational sermons embellished with the taste and talent of a scholar. Readers of choice literature should rejoice that these sermons have been put into permanent form and that there have been made available for the thinking public some of the best and most characteristic messages of a keen mind and a great heart.

It is our hope that this book will make for itself a wide circulation among our people so that these messages may continue to bless multitudes for many years to come.

—Pat M. Neff.

CONTENTS

INTRODUCTION

In offering these messages to the public, like Paul, the great Apostle, the author does not claim any "excellency of speech." There has been no effort at word parade, but a sincere effort to use every word at his command to make his thought clear, his passion emphatic, his pictures plain, and the truth easily understood.

These messages have been selected from a ministry of more than twenty-five years as pastor and pastor-evangelist. As does every preacher, he owes much to the many books which he has read and to the messages of others which he has heard with great delight and profit through the years. If he has failed to give credit where credit is due, it has been of the head and not of the heart.

He believes that these sermons and addresses will be found practical because all have been hammered out on the anvil of a practical, pastoral ministry. Each one has been used in his own church before being preached elsewhere. The purpose in each has been to secure a verdict in the hearts of his congregations for our Lord and Master. One of the most prized and appreciated compliments that has ever been paid the author was the expressed feeling on the part of some who have heard him deliver these sermons that "he would have made a good lawyer." Since this was his first ambition in life before the Lord made his perfect and acceptable will unmistakably clear to him, this compliment has always been most appreciated.

It has been the writer's keen desire to sell Jesus, his church, and the Cause of God, to those to whom he has ministered. To be a good salesman for Jesus has been the height of his ambition. He learned long ago that before one sells another on any matter he must first sell himself. To discover a great truth and let it surge in one's soul is the first prerequisite to effective preaching. However much the author has failed in his ministry, he has met this requirement: he has believed what he preached.

We are indebted to Dr. Robert G. Lee of Memphis, Tennessee, our college roommate, for valuable suggestions; to Miss Maud Peters of Tyler, Texas, for constructive criticism; to Miss Ella Mae Barron, our church secretary, for her faithful service as stenographer; to many others who have from time to time suggested that it would be profitable to God's cause to put these sermons in print.

Therefore, if some pastor's ministry shall be made stronger; if some Christian's heart shall beat a bit warmer; if some despondent soul shall find encouragement, and if some lost soul shall find Christ through the reading of these messages which have through the years become dear to our heart and which God has been pleased to bless in reaching many for Christ, and which the Holy Spirit has used to deepen a consecrated, spiritual life, the writer will be well repaid for all the hard work, time, and trouble that his first book of sermons has cost him.

PORTER M. BAILES.

First Baptist Church,
Tyler, Texas.

STEPS TO VICTORY

Texts: Ye are the salt of the earth. . . . Ye are the light of the world.—Matthew 5: 13, 14.

Go ye therefore, and teach all nations, . . . lo, I am with you alway.—Matthew 28: 19, 20.

The word "victory," as no other word, attracts the ear and thrills the heart of humanity. No word is more interesting than the word "success." No one has ever been rallied to a cause by talking defeat, failure, and bankruptcy. When our story is one of conquering, subduing, and overcoming, men will rally about our banners. It is our nature to want to be crowned; it is our desire to become triumphant and victorious. The words of mighty Cæsar, *veni, vidi, vici,* have become household words because they express, as few words ever uttered, the uppermost desire of every soul.

When Jesus came to his disciples and delivered his Great Commission, the radiance of a conqueror glowed on his face; the vision of a world kingdom stood before him; the ring and certainty of victory were in his voice, and the note of triumph was in his words. It was love commanding after conquering. There was nothing of hesitation. There were no "ifs" and "ands"; no surmises and uncertainties,—all was as clear as the noonday sun, as bright as a full moon in a cloudless sky, and as lucid as sparkling water. Listen, "All au-

(13)

thority hath been given unto me. . . . Go ye therefore, . . .
and, lo, I am with you alway." No conqueror ever spoke
with more assurance than when Jesus last addressed, on
this earth, his little handful of disciples.

Victory implies an adversary. Surely there are foes
a-plenty. Paul says: "We wrestle not against flesh
and blood, but against principalities, against powers,
against the rulers of the darkness of this world, against
spiritual wickedness in high places." No sane man can
doubt the seriousness of the times through which we
are passing. We are in a combat—one of the fiercest
and keenest ever entered—against sin and Satan in high
and low places, in the downs and outs, and in the ups
and outs. This is no sham-battle affair; it is a real warfare. If we win the victory over these fierce, relentless
and bitter enemies and deeply entrenched foes, we must
rely on divine and supernatural means.

However powerful the enemy, however deeply entrenched the foe, however bulwarked the adversary,
"the weapons of our warfare are not carnal but mighty
through God unto the casting down of strongholds."
These spiritual weapons have proved effective in the
past and will be successful now in this modern world if
we use them aright. One of the most thrilling stories
that has ever been told is how, with only spiritual means,
a victorious warfare by the early church was waged
against the mighty spiritual hosts of darkness. Without favorable public sentiment; with no great historical
background; with no great organization, and under bitter persecution and malice; against age-old customs
firmly entrenched, the early church won victory after
victory and went forth conquering and to conquer.

A conquering army must have a commander-in-chief.

Beyond any shadow of doubt, Jesus is the Master Commander—the Captain of our salvation. He is the Joshua of all ages. Maclaren says: "The Book of Acts is careful to point out how each step of the church's work was directed and commanded by Christ himself." Philip was definitely directed to join himself to the chariot of the eunuch; Peter in Joppa was commanded to go to the good Gentile Cornelius; Paul was prevented by the Spirit of Jesus from going into Bithynia and directed by a man in a vision to go into Macedonia.

In this, our modern warfare, what a Commander Jesus is! He knows both the strength and the weakness of his adversary; he knows the capacity and the power of his own forces; he knows the human heart as none other who ever lived. He is touched with the feeling of our infirmities and was tempted in all points, yet without sin. He is a leader whom to follow one never goes astray; a commander whom to obey, one never loses a battle.

In this warfare the Master Commander has given the pre-eminent promise, "Lo, I am with you alway." They tell us that the personal presence of Julius Cæsar transformed every common soldier into a hero. Did it ever dawn on you that Christ is more—far more—concerned about the success of his Cause and the Victory of his soldiers than we could possibly be? We are not fighting under the command of one who is indifferent or callous or professional. Our Commander is not a hireling. The shout of victory in the camp of his followers brings far more joy to his bleeding, broken heart than to any other heart however warmly it might have beaten for God's Cause. Surely, with this pre-eminent promise, we can and should say with Count Zinzendorf: "I have but one passion. It is for Jesus. Jesus only."

The first step to victory is to sell ourselves on the worthwhileness, the vital value, and the supreme importance of Christian work. No man has ever supported wholeheartedly any proposition that he did not think was worth while. You will never rally men around a cause which they do not deem of vital value. People do not give themselves to a work of doubtful importance. We must resell our people on the fundamental importance of the Church and its program, upon our missionary program and its objectives. The sharp point of this question—"Is it worth while?"—should pierce each heart of every believer.

Let me ask, then, Is salt worth while in this world of decay and dissolution? Jesus said, "Ye are the salt of the earth; ye are the light of the world." Is salt necessary in order to keep flesh pure and wholesome? Is light worth while in this world of darkness and ignorance? Could we get along at all without light? Is it a necessity to our well-being and happiness? Do the church and its work and influence make a contribution to our homes, to our business, to our social life, and to our individual lives? Does it make life nobler and happier? Does it stabilize business, purge social life, and undergird our homes? Has Russia lost anything in trying to do away with the church and in trying to build a civilization without faith in a deity? Is the preacher's contribution to society worth what it costs? Is his salary paid him charity or an investment? If I believed that my ministry as a minister did not make a vital, distinct, and helpful contribution to my community, I would get out of the ministry tomorrow and never preach again. Let me ask, Is the local church and its program of teaching, training, worship, prayer, and praise, worth while?

In answering this question, there are a great many things unseen and intangible but real and of the utmost importance. Mr. Lecky, in his *History of European Morals,* says: "The warming of Wesley's heart was a national epoch in the life of Briton and of far more importance to England than all the victories of Pitt by land or sea." An appraiser of that little Moravian gathering, in which John Wesley's heart was warmed by the Holy Spirit, would likely have overlooked the great significance of what was transpiring. It was intangible and unseen, but no meeting of Parliament in a decade was of such importance as that little meeting when Wesley's heart was warmed. John Wesley went out and preached a revival that saved England from a revolution that tore France to flinders.

If a Roman captain had been with Saul of Tarsus when he met his Master face to face and had become imbued with spiritual dynamite, this captain would likely have reported that nothing of serious consequences occurred that day. But something came to pass that day that was destined to shake the Roman Empire from center to circumference. Again, if some one had been in Colchester, England, when a young man on a cold, snowy day, heard a layman stammer out a sermon, he would probably have said, "Nothing happened here worthy of note." But a spiritual life was started and a force begotten that all the world was to hear about a century afterward—for Charles Haddon Spurgeon was born again that day.

If any one doubts the worthwhileness and importance

of the missionary program of the church and its objective, he should look to the root and branch from which we, the Anglo-Saxon race, sprang; the pit from which we were lifted. If you go back to our ancestors, you will stand face to face with a semi-savage pagan. Some of the names of their heathen gods have been given to the days of the week. Thus Sunday is their Sun-god; Monday, Moon-god; Tuesday, Teurico; Wednesday, Woden; Thursday, Thor; Friday, Friga, and Saturday, Saturn. These were the gods of our pagan ancestors.

What unholy boasting of our beautiful women we do! Their godless and vanity producing; their shameful beauty parades and revues are held almost everywhere showing our brunette beauties and blonde butterflies. We also boast of our brilliant-minded men and great geniuses. But back yonder before faithful missionaries came with the gospel to our ancestors, the Roman Servius said, "The stupidest and ugliest slaves in the market are from Briton." When I look on some specimens of American Anglo-Saxon, it is not at all difficult to believe that the "stupidest and ugliest slaves" were from Briton. But when I think of Edison, and Ford, and Burbank in the scientific field; of Emerson, the philosopher, of Wordworth, Milton, and Browning in the literary field; and of Spurgeon, Mullins, and Carroll, the great preachers and theologians, I wonder what power came and lifted the Anglo-Saxon race from such depths.

Some marvelous blessing came to the white race that other races did not receive. It has been said that one-third of the world's population, roughly speaking, is white; one-third yellow, and one-third brown; with one hundred million blacks thrown in for good measure.

But notice that this one-third white population controls seven-eighths of the earth's surface and others are even trying to control more. Why this predominance of world leadership among the white race? The natural gifts of the yellow man or of the brown man are just as great as those of the white man; and in some respects these gifts are greater. Why the great difference in world leadership? Can any one doubt that the ladder on which the white man climbed to world supremacy is the gospel of Christ which was brought to our semi-savage pagan ancestors by faithful missionaries? Did we ascend or descend in the scale of civilization by the power of the gospel? Did it give us wings or was it a weight? Did it make us better or worse? Did it prove a blessing or a curse? Considering all that the gospel has done for the white race, I can say with Paul, "I am not ashamed of the gospel of Christ: for it is the power of God unto salvation, to every one that believeth." Jesus Christ is no luxury but a vital and fundamental necessity. He is to the soul what bread is to the gnawing stomach; water to parched lips; a way to a lost man; truth to the ignorant; light to the blind, and a door of opportunity to the despairing. Christ is not excess baggage as some seem to think, but he is as necessary to high and holy living as air is to breathing lungs.

If preaching the gospel is not worth while, if the work and the services of the church are not worth while, if its program of missions is not worth while, if giving to God's Cause is not worth while, there is nothing in this world that we can give our thought, our time, our energy, our strength, or our means to that would be worth while.

Again, if we are to gain any great victory, we must win it on our knees. Prayer changes things. We preach ten days and pray ten minutes. The disciples prayed ten days and one preached a ten-minute sermon and the windows of heaven flew open. The Holy Spirit came and three thousand souls were saved. Let us consider the vital power of prayer.

First, no great moral or spiritual victory has ever been won aside and apart from prayer. The greatest date in all history is "When they had prayed." God gave his people the condition of all spiritual victories when he said, "If my people, which are called by my name, shall humble themselves, and pray, and seek my face, and turn from their wicked ways, then will I hear from heaven, and will forgive their sin, and will heal their land." Jesus prayed and the lame walked, the deaf heard, the dumb spoke, the dead arose, and the poor had the gospel preached to them. The dying thief prayed and the gates of glory opened to him and he became the "morning star of hope" for every sin-cursed soul. Stephen prayed and the glory of God shone in his face until his face looked like that of an angel. Persecuted pilgrims prayed until a new continent opened on which they planted the tree of religious liberty, which we trust will never die.

In *The Story of My Life and Work*, Booker T. Washington, that spiritual giant of the Negro race, states that the first time he realized that he and his mother were slaves was one morning when he was awakened from his sleep on a bed of rags on a clay floor by his mother kneeling over him and fervently praying that "she and her children might be free." Who knows but that God hastened the day of the abolition of slavery in answer to the prayers fervently made to him by these faithful "Black Mammies"?

Second, prayer is essential to victory because it gives God's people the right perspective. By it we can get the mind of God. Would you know something of the grace, the power, the poise, the patience, and the purity of Jesus? Then go to him as he withdraws from the crowd and spends a whole night alone on the mountain-side in prayer. He faces a crisis in his ministry. He must choose twelve men to be his special disciples. They must be men, dependable, trustworthy, and faithful. They must carry on and carry on under most strenuous circumstances after Jesus goes back to his Father. He needs in this crisis great spiritual wisdom and moral understanding. He must have the mind of God completely. He cannot afford now to allow his personal preferences to guide him. He must judge men, not as man judges man, by looking on the outward appearance, but he must judge the inner man and choose right. Therefore, bathing his soul in solitude, all night, in the quietness of a mountain-side, he spends it in prayer. The writer says: "When it was day, he called unto him his disciples: and of them he chose twelve, whom also he named apostles." And these twelve men left on the Kingdom and the world an indelible impress. Did ever twelve other men mean more to God's Kingdom?

Look what a victorious life Paul lived! The first time we see the redeemed Saul he is on his knees. "Behold, he prayeth." He prayed almost everywhere and under all kinds of circumstances. He prayed on the seashore; prayed behind prison bars; prayed down by a riverside; prayed on the ship tossed by wind and wave;

and in houses of worship. He prayed for all things good; that Israel might be saved; that love might abound yet more and more; that God might open effectual doors of opportunity to him; and that all men might be filled with the fulness of God. No wonder his life was surcharged with spiritual power; no wonder he lifted the doors of a great empire off their hinges and planted churches that became centers of spiritual power and mighty forces for moral righteousness. If the devil trembles when he sees the weakest saint on his knees, he must have had a perfect rigor when he saw Paul get down on *his* knees.

Let God's people advance on their knees and all the devils in hell cannot defeat his mighty army. The great revival that came at the beginning of the nineteenth century had a background of prayer that is not generally known. President Washington said that he had more fears for the safety of the republic in the last years of the eighteenth century than in the darkest hour of the revolutionary war. The closing years of the eighteenth century have been described as "the lowest water-mark of the lowest ebb-tide of spiritual life in the history of America." Our schools and universities were hotbeds of infidelity. In 1792 only one student in Princeton University claimed to be a Christian. The western frontier witnessed a complete moral breakdown. Read the *Out-Laws of Cave-In Rock* and see how the Harp brothers committed in Tennessee and Kentucky the most brutal murders that were ever heard of up to that day. It was the boast of infidels that the church would not survive two generations. Payne, the author of the infidel's Bible, declared "he would tear down in a single generation what it took the church eighteen centuries to build up."

The Christian forces had their backs to the wall. They faced the issue—Christ or chaos. They tell us that it is darkest just before dawn. So a group of twenty-three ministers in the eastern states sent out a letter asking that the first Tuesday in each quarter be set apart as a day of prayer. A covenant was entered into in the western states to spend the third Saturday of each month in prayer and fasting. Others pledged to spend a half hour at sunset on Saturday and a half hour at sunrise on Sunday in prayer, for the power of the Holy Spirit. Prayer societies were formed. Aaron and Hur societies met to support the pastors.

They prayed. "When they had prayed," God did not fail them. The power of infidelity was completely broken. Wicked and lawless communities, where brawls and fights were most common, were transformed into peaceful, godly neighborhoods. Bible, tract, and missionary societies were organized; denominational papers were established; seminaries were founded and all the church work took on new life. Hosts of people were won to the Lord and added to the churches as they were saved. A new day of victory dawned upon America "when they had prayed."

How we need today the spirit of prayer and intercession to come upon us! We say we live in an age of reason, when one spark from a fanatic's pistol in 1914 set the world on fire. It looked as if it might be repeated many times since; we say it is an age of wealth and yet every nation is tottering under a burden of debt that threatens its existence and there have been bread lines, doles, and relief such as the world has never known before. We say it is an age of benevolence, and yet half the human race is rotting in diseases, without access to a physician. If the world ever needed a revival to sweep over it, the hour is now. When we pray, these cold hearts will be warmed and these indifferent spirits kindled with holy zeal.

The third step to victory is an organization clothed with power from on high and conscious of the personal presence of Jesus Christ. No sane man will belittle the vital importance of organization in the church. Christ certainly had his little group of disciples organized. Peter, James, and John must have composed the executive committee. The quiet and faithful Andrew was the contact man. Judas was the treasurer, and when he failed, they chose Matthias to fill his *"office."* The church had not gone very far until they felt the need of deacons and seven men "of good report, full of the Holy Spirit and wisdom" were elected. The Apostles gave themselves to "prayer and the ministry of the word." The church is nothing more nor less than a spiritual organization used and directed of the Holy Spirit to do the will of God on earth. Every Christian ought to be in closest fellowship with some church. Every soldier should don the uniform of baptism and every worker should be busy in the vineyard of the Lord.

The fourth step to victory is the keen sense of stewardship. God's program to finance his Kingdom is not a money-raising scheme but a soul-growing and character-developing program. He wants us to be like himself—great givers. Paul said, "I do not seek yours but you." We can and should seek men through what they have. The greatest wrong any preacher can do a

church is to fail in developing the sense of stewardship. To bless a church is to create a generous, liberal
spirit in the church. God does not care about the gift
as such, but he does care mightily about the giver.

In a Baptist church, there are no dues as a lodge, no
assessments as taxes, but there should be from all—every
member—tithes and offerings. This is the simple principle laid down by the matchless Missionary when he
said, "Upon the first day of the week let each one of
you lay by him in store, as he may prosper." It is far
more than our duty to give. It is a high privilege and
a great opportunity to give; for,

> To give is to live,
> To deny is to die.

Giving becomes a joy to those who know something
of the cause for which they give and who give in the
name of Christ. What one gives depends not on
the amount he has but on the degree of his love for
the Lord and for his Cause. One's giving depends on
whether he is a *pond* or a *puddle*. The puddle soul
is the small, niggardly soul that never feels the pull
and urge of a great cause. But the pond is that soul
which is moved by the pull of the moon and is stirred
by the tides and is swayed by the storms and winds.
Pond or puddle, which are you? A keen sense of stewardship is a prerequisite to victory both by the church
and in the heart of the individual.

What a great joy when victory is won in our own
individual lives or in our homes! There came to my
study some years ago, a young mother carrying in her
arms, daintily dressed, a beautiful brown-eyed ten-
months-old baby girl. This young mother was all aglow

with her joy and zeal in the work of the Lord. She was superintendent of the Beginners Department and president of the Woman's Missionary Society in her church.

The first time I saw this young woman she and her young husband came to my study, stranded. They had shipped what little household effects they had to another town and they were "thumbing" their way. They were dejected and despondent. They came for help and something to eat. I laid on their hearts the best I could the cause of God. Neither of them was a Christian. We prayed together and then provided for them a meal or two. The way opened for them. It was very difficult sailing for a while. But finally the sea grew calmer and winds more favorable. I baptized both of them the same night. They now have regular employment and a respectable living. With a glow on her face that I shall never forget, she said that "from the time they accepted Christ until that day when she visited in my study with the ten-months-old baby, they had never been in want." They had not always had work, but they had never been in want. All was so different. Christ gave her a home, a means of honorable living, and the home had been blessed with a beautiful baby. All had changed because she had changed. She had found the Lord and the Lord had blessed abundantly. She expressed a wish to tithe, but her husband thought it was too much to give the Lord. Too much to give God when God had given them all that they possessed that was worth while! How ungrateful some are for God's great mercies!

When we think of what God has done for us, we ought to be willing to be used of him in any way he wills, knowing that his will is good, acceptable, and perfect. To be mastered by the will of God is to be lifted from the deepest depths to the highest heights. I heard a story of Gypsy Smith, Sr. He has in his beautiful home in England an old pruning knife which he keeps lying in the window of his living-room. This man who has been many times around the world; this man who has drawn to his services thousands on thousands; this man who has been entertained by the notables the world over says when he begins to feel a little proud, cocky, and puffed up, he goes back to his home and, taking down the old pruning knife, says to himself, "Old man, this is what you came from. This is where the Lord found you,—with that knife making clothes pins for a miserable living. There is nothing in you to be proud of. You owe it all to God's tender grace and great mercy." And so do we all!!

WILL HELL EVER BE VACATED?

TEXTS: If the righteous scarcely be saved, where shall the ungodly and the sinner appear?—1 Peter 4: 18.

In hell he lift up his eyes, being in torments.—Luke 16: 23.

The doctrine of hell to any unsaved soul is the most objectionable and disagreeable doctrine of any in all God's Word. It looks as if the idea of hell has about faded out of the mind of the general public. To announce that one is to preach on hell causes a smile to play over an audience. Many of our great daily newspapers refer to it in sarcasm. By many it is no longer taken seriously. We think we have outgrown the idea along with that of witches and ghosts, and we have hell everywhere but in our thought.

Whatever present-day thought may be on hell, the Bible teaches this doctrine as plainly and as distinctly as any doctrine it sets forth; Jesus certainly taught future punishment in parable and statement. In the story of Dives and Lazarus, he sets forth the idea without equivocation. This is all I care to know. If it is in God's Word and if Christ taught it, that settles the question with me.

Some "ifs." If there is no hell hereafter, as many profess to believe and teach, what are you going to do with hell here and now? Somebody has well said that we are not rewarded so much for our righteousness as by our righteousness. The greatest reward for right living is a righteous life. Again, we are not punished so much for our sins as by our sins. The greatest punishment that we can have is a sinful soul. If a soul, sin-diseased, rotten, filled with remorse, regret, and sorrow is not hell, I do not know what it would take to constitute it.

Again, if the state has a right to punish its incorrigible citizens, then God has an equal right to allow incorrigible souls to suffer in an endless eternity. If the idea of hell is wrong, then our whole civilization is based on the wrong principle—which principle is that society has a right to be protected from its incorrigible and lawless members.

Some say that God is too merciful and too loving to allow one to suffer the torments of an endless hell. But they forget that God has done all he can do to reach the lost and undone soul. His love is far beyond any compassion or emotion of man. But there are some things God cannot and will not do. He cannot make two hills without a valley and he will not save one against his will. "Whosoever will let him take the water of life freely." God has never yet and will not send one single soul to hell. He wills that all shall be saved. Hell was not made for men but for the devil and his angels. "Depart from me, ye cursed, into everlasting fire, PREPARED FOR THE DEVIL AND HIS ANGELS" (Matt. 25:41). If one chooses to serve the devil here, is there anything inconsistent in his spending an eternity in the place prepared for the devil yonder? Dives did not charge God with sending him to torment. Those at the judgment seat will cry for the rocks and mountains to fall on them and hide them from the wrath of the Lamb. Nobody knows, more than a soul steeped in sin, whose conscience is aroused, the terrible guilt that such a soul feels. Each will feel the guilt and responsibility resting upon his soul and that thought will add to the torments of hell. To know that one's sorrow is because of one's neglect adds tremendously to the sorrow. And to realize that "I am here because of my foolishness" will add to the flames of hell.

Our text gives us the irremediable doom of the lost. If the righteous are scarcely saved, where shall the ungodly and the sinner appear? The door by which one enters life is narrow, the way of life is strait—difficult to stay on. If the man who seeks and strives to do God's will, who does the best he knows how to meet the conditions of salvation; if such a one is scarcely saved, where shall the ungodly—the man whose life is void of all that is holy and divine—the Sabbath desecrater, the unbeliever, the drunkard, the covetous, the liar, the thief—the sinner—the man who has missed the mark in this life—where will he appear? That's a question that God is asking us to answer. Where would you place such? Whose group will he show up in? Since death works no transformation in the soul, he will show up in the same group in which he was found in this world.

Some will be saved, but as by fire. Their works will be burned up—their life in this world lost—their souls saved but lives lost. If any man build on wood, hay, or stubble, he shall suffer loss but he himself shall be saved. The fact is that none—not even the most saintly —has any cause to boast of any margin on salvation by good works. Jesus says that it is like a servant who comes in and does his duty to his master, "So likewise ye, when ye shall have done those things commanded you, say, We are unprofitable servants: we have done that which was our duty to do." After you have kept the Ten Commandments, rendered your tithe to God, served the Lord with an undivided love and loved your neighbor as yourself, then you shall say, "I am an unprofitable servant." Where can there be boasting? Where is there any margin? The more consecrated, the more unworthy we feel. The more wicked and degenerate of heart, the more men are given to unholy boasting. If the righteous scarcely be saved, where shall the sinner and the ungodly appear?

An answer to this question should send chills up our spines. It is an answer that should put fear and trembling in our souls. Where did Dives, the handsomely dressed, the well-fed, the prosperous but impenitent sinner, appear? God says, "In hell he lift up his eyes, being in torments, . . . and he cried and said, . . . have mercy on me, . . . for I am tormented in this flame." Where did the five foolish virgins, who slumbered and slept and failed to make ready for the bridegroom, appear? God says, "And the door was shut." Then they cried, "Lord, Lord, open to us." An answer that sent a chill to the depths of their souls came back, saying, "I know YOU not."

Where did the unprofitable servant who wrapped his Lord's money in a napkin, laid it away and was content to do nothing, appear? God says: "Cast ye the unprofitable servant into outer darkness: there shall be weeping and gnashing of teeth."

Where will those appear who failed to visit, feed,

clothe, and give drink to the Christ in others? God says they shall hear this terrible doom, "Depart from me, ye cursed, into everlasting fire, prepared for the devil and his angels." And where will those on the left hand at the judgment seat appear? God says, "These shall go away into everlasting punishment."

Where did the tares appear that the enemy sowed among the wheat and that became a hindrance—choking out and retarding the growth of the wheat? God says, "Gather up first the tares and bind them in bundles to burn them." Where did the chaff that was separated from the wheat on the threshing floor by the judgment fan appear? God says, "The chaff, he will burn with unquenchable fire."

There's a picture for the ungodly soul to gaze upon. Fire unquenchable. The anguish of torments. Punishment everlasting—punishment without let-up or end. WEEPING. Did you ever hear anybody really weep?

It was my sad duty some years ago to conduct the funeral of a murderer and suicide. Circumstantial evidence pointed to him unmistakably as the murderer. He had been arrested and let out on bond. The day of the trial came. That morning, he arose and after writing a note to his family, sent a bullet through his brain. The bereaved family asked me to be with them in the last sad services. At the funeral I said that if I had the privilege I would read personally to each one of the bereaved ones certain portions of God's Word. Not having that personal privilege, I would read publicly. So I read some passages that have become favorites of mine for times of sickness and sorrow. It looked as if every passage read condemned the one whose body was lying there with the blue bullet hole in his temple.

Really that day I let God conduct that funeral. Then came the family to take the last look at husband's and father's body. As they stood looking, I have never heard before nor since such deep groans and such bitter weeping. I asked the undertaker years afterwards if he remembered the occasion. He said he did distinctly. As I listened to that family weep, weep as those who have no hope for their loved ones, weep with a heart that seemed ready to break with sorrow, I said, "If that is hell, God have mercy, I don't want it."

GNASHING OF TEETH. This means madness. Weeping is the symbol and sign of sorrow, but gnashing of teeth is the sign of madness. If God's Word is true, if Christ was sincere in his teaching, the ungodly—those who forget God, despise and neglect his laws and commandments—and the sinner will open their eyes in hell, stand in outer darkness midst weeping and gnashing of teeth. Jesus was no fanatic but most sane. All he taught that we can prove in this world has been proved to be sane, sensible, and wise. Why not be warned by his teaching on the condition of the lost soul in the other world?

But some say that hell will be vacated; that God will finally restore all things to himself. But let us ask, "Will the sinner, the ungodly, the doomed, the damned, the cursed, come back from hell?" Some teach that the dark caverns of blasphemy will some day become chambers of silence where sound and echo are heard no more. They believe, so they say, that hell will be vacated and a sign, "FOR RENT" or "TO LET" will be hung over its black gates; that every creature—man and fallen angels, with all the imps of hell—will be restored to heaven, to holiness, to happiness, and in perfect unity and harmony with God.

Let us consider. God's Word speaks of three deaths. The first death is spiritual death, which is the separation of the soul from God. This came upon man when our first parents ate of the forbidden fruit. God said, "Ye shall not eat of it, neither shall ye touch it, *lest ye die*." They ate of it and were separated from God and driven out of the garden lest they eat of the tree of life and live forever in this body. Always afterwards man must have a mediator, a kinsman redeemer, a Boaz. So God says, "As through one man sin entered into the world, and death through sin; so death passed unto all men, for that all sinned." But from this spiritual death, there is a comeback. By faith in a living redeemer, men rise from this spiritual death into a new life. "If by the trespass of the one the many died, much more did the grace of God, and the gift by . . . one man, Jesus Christ, abound unto the many." I do not hesitate to say that you can rise from this spiritual' death by faith in the shed blood of Jesus and walk in newness of life.

But the Bible speaks of another death—physical death. This death occurs when the soul is separated from the body. Seth died, Kenan died. "And he died" is written seven times in the fifth chapter of Genesis. "It is appointed unto men once to die." Men do not fear physical death. They seek refuge from trouble, misfortune, and pain in it. But once this death has passed on one, there can be no change in the nature of one's condition. "As the tree falleth so shall it lie." If one dies the physical death without Christ, he remains lost; dying saved, he remains saved. What can separate us from the love of God in Christ Jesus? Certainly death cannot.

Another death is the death of a lost man. It is the deeper death and is called the "second" death. It is banishment from God into the lake of fire. This sentence of death comes from the judgment throne after the resurrection of the body. "If any was not found written in the book of life, he was cast into the lake of fire." The FEARFUL and UNBELIEVER along with the murderers, fornicators, and all liars "Shall have their part in the lake that burneth with fire and brimstone." This is a fearful statement, but from this decision there can be no appeal. Notice that the "fearful and unbelieving" are placed and catalogued with others—liars, murderers, and abominable. If the righteous are scarcely saved, where shall the sinner and the ungodly appear? One of the worst of sins is that of unbelief and mistrust.

Consider again. There will be no aids to salvation in hell. None will ever pray in hell an intercessory prayer such as Moses prayed for Israel; no one will wield a spiritual influence, nor sing a gospel song, nor preach a gospel sermon. All aids to salvation will sadly be missing. Satan and his demons are unrestrained; every vile and wicked influence is felt. No gospel appeal is ever made, no wooing spirit is ever felt, no gentle uplifting influence thrown around one. "When a wicked man dieth, his expectation shall perish." Surely without these aids to spiritual living, the soul whose doom is sealed would hope against hope.

The question is asked, "How shall we escape (from hell yonder), if we neglect so great salvation (here and now)?" What chance for escape would one have

if he should desire it? Because of its intense enmity,
hell would resist the slightest move toward God. The
fallen angels—quick, alert, powerful, and unrestrained
—would seize the fugitive and drag him back. How
would any one escape? Certainly not by one's own
power. No man ever yet lifted himself over a fence
by pulling at his bootstraps. How would you escape?
Not by the grace of God. Today is the day of salvation. Now is the acceptable time. How shall we escape
the pull, the anguish, and torment of hell if we neglect
so great salvation here and now?

Hell will never be emptied because there is a fixed
and IMPASSABLE GULF. That gulf begins in this life.
It is the chasm between the righteous and the ungodly.
Years ago, two boys were bosom friends and constant
companions. They grew up together, went to school
together, and became almost inseparable. But the time
came when their lives took a decided turn. One turned
toward God and became a minister; the other turned
more from God and became most ungodly. There was
no concern in his soul for the higher things and seem-
ingly no interest in things divine. There's a gulf between the two which is almost impassable now. When
this gulf strikes the death line, it will become fixed and
impassable. The fixed and impassable gulf between
Dives and Lazarus after death was only a continuation
of the gulf which existed between them in this world—
the rich man faring sumptuously every day and the
poor man who lay at his gates desiring to be fed from
the crumbs which fell from his table. Jesus was trying
to describe an inward condition by terms of outward
circumstances. However great the gulf might be between them physically, there was a far greater gulf

between them spiritually. The fixed and impassable gulf forbids hell ever being vacated.

Again, SALTED WITH FIRE is a horrible idea that the reader may take for what it is worth, but the writer finds it significant. Jesus said, "Every one shall be salted with fire" (Mark 9: 49). Salt preserves and fire destroys and consumes. The process is one strange to the carnal mind, but in this metaphor we have the idea of being eternally preserved and eternally destroyed. Add to this horrible idea that of acute pain and the picture is horribly complete. Apply salt to a burned place and if one does not dance a jig and sob a sigh, I do not know what it would take to cause acute pain.

But some one asks, Did not Christ preach to the spirits in prison? Some think that while his body lay in the grave, "He descended into hell" and preached to the spirits who entered prison during the flood. If Jesus did that, we have no record or intimation where any imprisoned spirit repented and turned to God. Christ preached to these spirits, but he did it before they entered the prison. He went while Noah was building the ark and strove with them. Every piece of timber Noah fitted into the ark was a sermon, and every nail was a call to repentance. God said, "My spirit shall not always strive with man." When God closed the door of the ark on Noah, his family and the twos of all the living creatures, these millions of rebellious souls were doomed and their curse sealed. That door of judgment was not opened until the visitation of his wrath was complete. I would earnestly warn any one against the futile hope of a second chance in the other world.

There must be a promotion or debasement awaiting every soul after physical death. As there is a second and higher life, so there is a second and deeper death. As after this higher life, there is no more death; so after this deeper death, there is no more life. Many of the ungodly in dying have caught a glimpse of this deeper death before passing from this earth. Many, too, of the righteous have caught glimpses of the higher life and heard the songs of heavenly hosts before passing through this veil of tears. One, ungodly, while dying, cried, "I am about to take a leap in the dark." No ray of light pierced the blackness of the pit. It looked black and bottomless.

How close to hell are you? "There is only a step between me and death," said David. Only a thin veil stands between any man and eternity. Some one has said, "Wrap the left ventricle of the heart around your forefinger, hold it arm's length and so thin is that membrane that you cannot tell with the sight of the natural eye whether there is aught wrapped around your finger." Prick this membrane with the point of a cambric needle and instant death results.

How brittle and slender is the cord of life! It can be severed by a small pen-knife. It doesn't take a shotgun or a bolt of lightning to break the cord of life, but it can be snapped by a germ that you can't see with your natural eye. A story is told of one, a noted unbeliever. During a severe thunderstorm, he walked out in his yard and dared God to strike him with a thunderbolt. Lightning was flashing all about him. His friends, who saw him, said, "Man, come inside and quit defying God." It angered him and again he turned his impious face toward heaven and with clinched fists cried, "I dare God to strike me with a bolt of lightning." His friends plead with him to cease playing the fool and come in and be quiet. Again he challenged God as the forked, zigzag lightning played about him. But about that time, something stung him on the hand. He scratched it and took little notice of it. But soon it began to sting and burn. Soon his hand began to swell and the swelling went into his arm. His fever arose and he became sick unto death. Soon his body swelled and death came. In forty-eight hours he was in his grave. The doctors pronounced it erysipelas. But neighbors believed it was God. God did not have to strike this puny being with lightning. All he had to do was to commission one of his tiny insects to carry the germ of poison and deposit it in the blood stream. Oh! how easily snapped is the brittle cord of life!

How near death and tragedy are you? Some years ago, the author was conducting a revival meeting in the mountains. He was guest in a home close by the summer hotel. As he returned one evening, he was asked if he knew that a boy had fallen over the precipice. The sad news shocked him and he went in to look at the boy's bruised and broken body. Imagine, if you can, the ache at his heart when he heard what had taken place the evening before. A group of boys, of which the deceased was a member, had come to spend a few weeks camping in the mountains. Just the evening before, they passed down the road hollering. As they passed the site of another group of campers they shouted, "Hurrah! we are on our way to hell!" The leader of the second camping group and his associates were cooking their evening meal. As the first group passed and shouted, "Hurrah! we're on our road to hell," the associate said, "They might be a little closer than they think." The next morning, this leader of the second group went to their camp and found them playing cards and using the most vulgar and vile profanity. He spoke to them and said, "Boys, I wouldn't do that." They gave him the "horse laugh." Soon the leader turned and went back to his camp and said, "Boys, we must move. It won't do to stay so close to those other boys." They broke camp and moved on.

That afternoon, the first group of boys were sitting around the hotel and one suggested that they go mountain climbing. But the boy whose body was crushed said he would not go. They plead with him and begged him, but he stedfastly refused and did not go as the others went. Soon after they started, he changed his mind and followed them. One boy had climbed the head of the precipice and returned to the foot when he heard a terrible noise of falling. Looking up he saw this boy falling over almost a sheer precipice of five hundred feet. When his body reached the bottom, it was broken and bruised and bleeding. When those boys the evening before had shouted, "Hurrah, we're on our road to hell," this boy didn't know he was within twenty-four hours of a tragic death. How close are you?

How near death are you? Some years ago a young man in a distant city had purchased a motorcycle of which he was very proud. He had employment at a lumber yard. The first day he came to work on his beautiful new motorcycle, he was eager for quitting time, so he might again enjoy a ride on his beautiful new machine. The time to quit finally came. He hurriedly rolled his motorcycle out, and mounting it, and starting out, he looked back and said, "Good-bye, boys! I'll ride into home or hell by six-fifteen." While traveling at a rapid rate of speed, he crashed into an automobile at a street crossing and by six-fifteen the poor deluded soul breathed his last.

If the righteous scarcely are saved, where shall the ungodly and sinner appear? I bring you good news of glad tidings which are unto all men,—"He that believeth and is baptized shall be saved; but he that believeth not shall be damned." To be saved is as simple as calling—"for whosoever shall call upon the name of the Lord shall be saved." Won't you call and live?

O sinner friend, you might think that in this message I have tried to scare you into the Kingdom. But I have sought only to present sober facts as found in and deducted from God's Word. It is utterly impossible to scare one into the Kingdom. If the writer could scare people into the Kingdom, he would willingly spend every hour of every day in such service. While no one can be frightened into the Kingdom, if any one is made to think on his way by what has been written, we shall be happy. Let me ask, where would you be now but for the grace of God? Will you not settle this important question at once and for all by calling on the name of the Lord?

GOD'S MUST FOR ALL MEN

TEXT: For we must all be made manifest before the judgment-seat of Christ. . . . Knowing therefore the fear of the Lord, we persuade men.—2 Corinthians 5: 10, 11.

Paul, the greatest of all missionaries, writes. He suffered as few men have been called on to suffer for the cause of Christ. He made three great, glorious, history-making, epochal, missionary journeys. He stood fiery trials, endured heart-sickening tribulations and five times his back was beaten bloody and blue. Why! Why! did he go on? He tells us here: "Knowing therefore the fear of the Lord, we persuade men." The fear of the Lord drove him on to reach the last lost man without God and without hope. "The fear of the Lord" explains why he endured the fierce persecutions, the stonings, the shipwrecks, the scourging, the weariness, and pain.

Read his perils! He was in perils of waters, of robbers, of his own countrymen, by the heathen, in the city, in the wilderness, in the sea, and among false brethren. It seems that there was no safe place anywhere for this man with the dynamite of God. Why did he go on? This question again crowds to the front. He tells us again, "Knowing therefore the fear of the Lord, we persuade men."

Always and in everything, the purpose of his jour-

neys, the passion of his heart, and the compelling motive
of his soul were to win men to Christ. There were two
great, outstanding motives which moved him: One,
the glory of God,—"Whether therefore ye eat, or
drink, or whatsoever ye do, do all to the glory of God."
This moved him, this passion consumed, this zeal fired
him. The other motive was persuading men for Jesus.
Knowing that the man without Christ is in imminent
danger of an eternal hell, and of the wrath of God,
and that here and now his soul is lost and undone, he
was compelled to go out and persuade men. This is the
secret supreme of his wonderful life,—a life filled so
full of soul-winning missionary labors.

Every other preacher who feels in his soul the surg-
ing of this passion must go on preaching the unsearchable riches of God's great grace in Christ Jesus. The
pay, the parsonage, the place, the people, make little
difference. The work is all one. Down in the heart
of every God-called preacher is the feeling of the prince
of preachers, "Woe is me if I preach not the gospel."
That is why so many preachers go on receiving pit-
tances and salaries that are meager and poor. That is
why they are willing to be lied about, to be abused, and
to forego for themselves and their families many of
the comforts of life which might be theirs in any other
profession. The secret is in this, right here, "Knowing therefore the fear of the Lord, we persuade men."

The fear of the Lord comes from the certainty of the
judgment. The "therefore" refers back to the statement, "We must all be made manifest before the judgment-seat of Christ." The judgment—the great assize
—puts fear in the hearts of men. When Paul before
Felix reasoned of righteousness, of temperance, and

the JUDGMENT to come, he trembled; he felt uneasy; he quailed; his soul sank within him. Like Belshazzar, his thoughts troubled him. The thought that out yonder we must face the record of our sinful living, review again the ugly and base things and answer for our foolish and insane sins, this thought should bring fear into the soul of any man. Bring any man who is not right with God face to face with the thought of the judgment of God, and his soul will quail. He will tremble.

"We must all appear before the judgment-seat of Christ" is the only thing God says all men must do. I have heard some state that God says "All men must die," but nowhere in the Book does he say that. It would not be true to facts if he did say it. All men have not died and all men will not die. Enoch did not die, but went home with God one day and never came back. Elijah did not die, but was translated in a whirlwind. Moses had a strange death. We do not know what blessing was bestowed on him on Mount Nebo. The saved here on earth when Christ comes back to receive his bride will not die. They shall be caught up together with him in the clouds and escape death. God says, "It is appointed unto men once to die, but after this the judgment." It is the usual and general thing for men to die but not all will die. But God does say that "We must all be made manifest before the judgment-seat of Christ," and this means exactly what it says.

God in his Book seldom uses the word "must." He is not a God of compulsion but a God of persuasion. He does not conscript but pleads for volunteers. He does not force men and women; they must willingly offer

themselves. Love never compels, but woos and wins.
There are conditions that must be met in his plan of
salvation, but one always has a choice. There is only
one way to enter the Kingdom, and if we would enter,
we "must" be born again. There is only one remedy
for sin, and if Christ would save men from sin he
"must" be lifted up as Moses lifted up the serpent in
the wilderness. There is only one name given among
men without blemish, and if we would be made whole
this name in its full significance "must" become ours.
Every "must" that God uses in the Book is in connection with his plan of redemption except one, and this
one "must" for all men refers to the judgment-seat of
Christ. Every knee shall bow and every tongue shall
confess some day to the Lord of lords and the King of
kings.

There are very few things absolutely certain in this
world. It is not at all certain that the sun will rise
tomorrow and flood the world with light. It has never
yet failed in these thousands of years to do so. But
one day, we will wake up in eternity—the endless ages
of eternity will be upon us. The moon will be turned
to blood and the sun will be as black as sackcloth.
Again, it is not certain that you will find your home
as you return from some journey. So many things may
happen to it. Some malicious soul might stick dynamite under it and blow it, in a moment's time, into a
thousand pieces; or a strong wind might lift it and
crush it as an eggshell. Fire, like a mighty monster,
might eat out its framework and consume its walls and
roof and leave your home a pile of ashes and charcoal.
It is not at all certain that you will rise tomorrow morning for your day's work or play. Many shall die as

the clock ticks away the moments of time during the night. Many shall be called to meet God before the morning light breaks again. The wreath of mourning might be hung on your door by the hand of the mortician tomorrow morning. Where will the wreath of mourning be placed next in any community? Who knows but it might be on *your* door. The most uncertain quantity in our plans is the thing we count on most —life. There is but a step between any of us and death. That step becomes shorter as civilization becomes more complex. There is only one thing certain, only one fact assured, only one matter settled—we must all appear before the judgment-seat of Christ.

There is no "either—or" here. Men have their choice about many other things in this world. Adam and Eve had the choice of obeying either the command of God or the voice of the serpent. That same privilege of choosing between good and evil is ours. Pilate could say in his puzzled and troubled soul, "What then shall I do unto Jesus who is called Christ?" He chose to let him be crucified. That question will be reversed at the judgment, not what shall *I* do with Jesus but what will *Jesus* do with me? We may accept or reject Christ, as we choose. It is up to you to live either the life of the righteous, whose path is a dawning light, or the life of the ungodly, whose way shall perish. You can die either the death of the saint, which is precious in the sight of the Lord, or of the sinner, who goes out and, like Judas, "it was night." You choose whether you will spend eternity in hell or in heaven, and it is up to you to choose between serving God or the devil. It is yours to choose whether you will follow Christ in beautiful baptism or refuse complete obedience to him. It is yours to say whether your life will count for God or for Satan. But there is one matter over which you have no choice—you must appear before the judgment-seat of Christ. That matter is settled and fixed finally; we have no choice there.

All men everywhere, of every race and tongue, of every tribe and nation, of every clime and color, *must* one day appear before the judgment-seat of Christ. When the trumpet of the Lord shall sound and time shall be no more, and the dead are raised and the sea shall give up its dead—in a moment, in the twinkling of an eye—when this old world is on fire, then God's "must" for all men will become effective.

Men have committed the most heinous crimes and were never arrested. They were never forced to face the judgment-seats of this world. Always criminals try to cover up every lead and leave no marks or signs of identity behind them. Not often do men escape the judgment of this world, but sometimes they do. But there is one Court and one Judge that all must face. The perfect crime has never yet been committed and never will be so long as God is God and man is man.

The story is told of Ruth Wheeler, who one morning left her home in a great city to seek work and never came back. Some days after her disappearance, a burnt torso was found in a basket on a fire escape. Peace officers, who can be most effective when they try, secured all possible evidence. They saved bits of the dress and jewelry and other evidences. A man, Albert Wolter, was finally arrested. The day of the trial came. The accused man was there and the sister of Ruth Wheeler was placed in the witness chair. The attorney had the little bits of evidence in a little box, and his plan was first to identify the torso as being the mangled and burnt body of Ruth Wheeler. He would hold up bits of the dress and say to the sister, "Did you ever see cloth like this before?" She would answer, "Yes." "Where did you see it?" and she would say, "Ruth wore a dress like that the morning she left, never to come back." Thus the prosecuting attorney did with rings and bracelets. Then he called the sister from the witness chair and addressed the jury, saying, "Gentlemen of the jury, I have shown you beyond a shadow of doubt that this burnt torso is Ruth Wheeler's body. This torso contained a hand that held in it six human hairs. These six human hairs were burned on each end. Under the microscope it is easily seen that these six human hairs are not hers. They are decidedly a different texture and color from hers. But comparing them with the hair of another, they are the same texture and color as the hair of this man, Albert Wolter. Here, Gentlemen of the jury, is the brutal murderer of this young woman."

So suddenly and unexpectedly did this attorney prove his case that Albert Wolter, the accused criminal, flushed a crimson red and confessed the whole brutal crime. As he struggled with the young woman, God had her reach out and reserve in her scarred hand the six hairs to bear conclusive testimony to the mad perpetrator.

What shall we do at God's judgment when the books are open and all the facts are in, when the secrets of the soul are laid bare, and when the accusing conscience stands pointing its finger? Ah! we shall cry for the rocks and the mountains to fall on us and hide us from the wrath of the Lamb! For we must all appear before the judgment-seat of Christ and give an account of the things done in the body. Knowing therefore the fear of the Lord, we persuade men.

THE CERTAINTY OF RELIGION. Notice the words used, "Knowing therefore the fear of the Lord." The writer here is not supposing, surmising, conjecturing, nor imagining; he says, "knowing." One may know in matters religious as certainly and as assuredly as in matters mathematical or scientific. How often the Apostle John uses this word, "know." "We know that we have passed from death unto life." "These things I have written unto you . . . that ye may know that ye have eternal life." "Hereby shall we know that we are of the truth." "We know that we are of God, and the whole world lieth in the evil one." There is no fact that we can be more assured of than the reality of God. I know that Christ died to save lost men, for he has saved me. I know there is a devil, for I have felt his downward pull on my soul. I know that God *is*, for I have had sweet communion with our Father who is in heaven.

Some years ago, a matchless preacher was conducting a series of meetings in a southern city. A most brilliant editor, who later became a college president, took it upon himself to cover this meeting for his paper. He was forty years old and an experienced newspaper man. During the series of meetings the brilliant editor found God. He was afterwards speaking to a Sunday school class of men and said, "Gentlemen, I have always thought that religion was a matter of the imagination. But I am here to tell you today, as an experienced newspaper man who can detect the true and the false, that religion is a reality. I have found the Lord and light has come into my soul." Sam Jones used to say that Christ made a new man out of him, and if folks didn't believe it, just ask his wife and neighbors. Give God a chance and he will prove himself to you beyond any shadow of doubt. Push up the shades of your soul and the light from heaven will shine in. Erect an altar and God will send his messenger to declare himself unto your soul. You may know! It is your privilege to know.

Knowing the vengeance and recompense of God, we persuade men. Listen to the Apostle Paul as he pleads, "Dearly beloved, avenge not yourselves but rather give place unto wrath; for it is written, Vengeance is mine; I will repay, saith the Lord." Have you ever realized that the Book teaches that God will some day repay all men out of Christ for every evil deed done and every idle word spoken on this earth? Vengeance must belong to God and he must repay, or else there is no justice here and will be none hereafter. God is not a mere mollycoddle; he is a judge and an avenger. Notice—God is omnipotent. He has all power and can enforce and execute every righteous decree and crush every soul rebellious to his will and reign. Yet some stand out against an omnipotent God, despise his only begotten Son, reject his gracious offers of peace and pardon and then expect God to deal with them as faithful servants at the judgment bar. If I know what justice is, that will not be done.

Other people dare to call the church, the bride of Christ, an old "hypocrite." If we should make such allegations against another man's wife, that man ought to make such a defamer swallow his words! Be careful how you rail against the bride of the Lamb. Never have I been guilty of such. The church is my spiritual mother. She has meant to me more than my mother in the flesh—and none ever had a more loving mother than I. My mother in the flesh, through suffering, brought me into the world, but my spiritual mother brought Christ to my heart. The life that my mother in the flesh gave me might have become a curse but for the life that my spiritual mother led me to in Christ Jesus. If the commands of the two mothers had ever conflicted—and I thank God they never did—I would have said to my dear mother in the flesh, I am sorry but I must do what my spiritual mother bids me.

> I love thy church, O God!
>   Her walls before Thee stand,
> Dear as the apple of Thine eye,
>   And graven on Thy hand.

Oh, what madness in men when they abuse and accuse and berate the church, the Lamb's bride and spiritual mother of millions. At the judgment bar where all men must some day appear, God will avenge, for he says, "I will repay."

Notice again, God is omniscient. He knows all the influences brought to bear upon one's soul for good or bad. He weighs our actions in the balances to the weight of a down of a feather. When one's life is completed; when the last word is spoken and the last deed is done; when your life is weighed on his unerring scales, without the imputed righteousness of Christ by faith, God will write over it, "MENE, MENE, TEKEL, UPHARSIN," —weighed! weighed! and found wanting! Yes, one can sneer, reject, spurn, scorn, and trample under foot the claims of the Son of God on his soul; he can lie to the preacher and say, "I will think about accepting Christ," as if Christ were a bargain sale proposition, making little difference whether he accepts him or not; and one can crucify him afresh and anew on a cross of indifference but remember this, God says, "Vengeance is mine; I will repay." Knowing that vengeance belongs to God, we persuade men.

Again, knowing that "whatsoever a man soweth that shall he also reap," we persuade men not to sow to sin. Knowing what the final results of all sin are; knowing that sin, hideous, slimy sin, brings forth death; that dainty, deadly sin brings wretchedness and misery; we persuade men not to sow to sin.

A story is told of a young man in Kentucky who had a neighbor with a beautiful, fertile, bluegrass farm. This neighbor kept his farm like a garden, free from any noxious weeds and grass. One night, in a mad rage at his neighbor, this young man took Johnson grass seed and scattered them all over the neighbor's beautiful farm. In a few weeks, the neighbor, walking over his farm, noticed sprig after sprig of this noxious grass. He wondered where it came from. He never found out.

Years came and went and this young man married the beautiful daughter of the neighbor; years slipped by again, and the neighbor died. Then when the estate was settled the farm with the Johnson grass seed was given to the young man's wife as her portion of her father's estate. Today that man is digging at the roots of a noxious grass that he sowed maliciously one night in a mad rage.

I know men who are digging at the roots of intemperance which have struck deep in their desires; others digging at the roots of profanity, the seed of which were sown years and years ago in the thoughtlessness and levity; and others digging at the roots of lust which many times have ruined a most promising life before middle age.

Knowing that sin brings forth death; the sin of neglect, the sin of covetousness; the sin of unbelief; the sin of indifference—all bring forth death—we persuade men. No one can nurse and play with this serpent by his fireside and in his living-room without reaping death somewhere, sometime. No one can practice this thing in late joy rides, in club houses, in tourist camps, or anywhere else without reaping the terrible harvest of death. Sow to the wind and a whirlwind is yours. Sow to the flesh and rotten flesh is yours. Leave off the sowing to evil and the harvest will never bother. But sow to sin and hell is yours.

We persuade men to do what? First, to be reconciled to God. "We are ambassadors for Christ, . . . be ye reconciled to God." "God was in Christ, reconciling the world unto himself." God the Father longs for the fellowship and companionship of all his prodigal sons. He is most anxious to have them return. There can be no reconciliation until sin has been removed. Thus we are God's ambassadors persuading men to be reconciled to God.

What sorrow when men refuse to be reconciled! One day, as Jesus stood on the Mount of Olives and looked across the valley at the beautiful city of Jerusalem and saw the Temple glittering in the morning sun, blinding tears coursed down his cheeks as he cried out, "O Jerusalem, Jerusalem, . . . how often would I have gathered thy children together, as a hen doth gather her brood, . . . and ye would not!" It broke his heart to know that he had come to his own and his own received him not. The saddest experience of a preacher or Christian worker is to see men go on to wreck and ruin after they have made every possible effort to win them and to reconcile them to God.

Second, we persuade men to forsake sin. Knowing the deceitfulness of sin, we plead with men before it is too late to come out of it. Sam Jones used to tell how, when he was a young man, Satan came one day and led him down a long, beautiful avenue and into a marvelous palace. He opened its doors and led Mr. Jones in. There in this beautiful palace of sin he sat in the chair of ease, lounged on the lounge of contentment, and played around the table of pleasure and sipped "the mocker" from the beautiful glass. Satan said, "I will give you all this if you will serve me." Mr. Jones replied that he would accept the offer.

So he played about the table, he sipped of the mocker, he reclined on the lounge of contentment and sat long in the chair of ease. One day he left and came back and the lounge of contentment was gone. Never again was he quite content in the palace of sin. Another day he left and came back and the chair of ease had been removed. Never again was he quite at ease in that palace. Again he left and came back and the table of pleasure was gone. Never afterwards was there any real joy in the palace.

From time to time he left and came back, and all the draperies and pictures and rugs were gone. Nothing was left but ugly, bare walls with an insipid sameness. Then again he left and came back and a window had been removed. Never after that was the palace

quite so light as before. From time to time he left and
came back and all the windows were gone, and every
door closed except one. He left through that door,
thank God, never to go back. But a friend of his lin-
gered in that palace until the last door was closed and
hope was forever gone. How terrible when the final
end came as he realized that "the wages of sin *is*
death"! Knowing the deceitfulness of sin's fine appearance, we persuade men to come out before it is
too late.

Third, we persuade men by preaching the unsearchable riches of Christ. "Unto me, who am less than the
least of all saints, is this grace given, that I should
preach among the Gentiles the unsearchable riches of
Christ," said Paul. How would you like to have wealth
that is inexhaustible? A treasure that never grew less;
a casket of jewels that could never be emptied? An
oil well that would never cease to flow? A bank account that could never be overdrawn? This is what
we are offered in spiritual riches in Christ. If you
would share in these unsearchable riches, follow the
blood-stream. It will lead you to Calvary.

In *Appleton's Fourth Reader,* there is a story, the
kind of which today is seldom found. The story is
that of a man in the pioneer days of our nation who
wished to migrate into another country. He sold all
his property and converted it into gold. He saddled
his horse and, placing his gold in saddle-bags, he and
his faithful dog, Fido, started to the new country. He
rode until noon and, coming to a shady nook, with a
bubbling spring, he decided to eat lunch. He unsad-
dled his horse, tethered it, and he, with his dog, ate
lunch. After lunch, he was drowsy and decided to take

a nap. He slept much longer than he planned, and was finally aroused by his dog licking him in the face. He saw the sun sinking rapidly in the west, and hurriedly he saddled his horse, mounted it and rode away. The dog ran forward and barked and ran back. He would run and jump for the bridle reins and run back. The man finally decided that his faithful dog was mad and being in a great hurry, the next time the dog came yelping and barking, he reared up on the man's leg and as he did so, the man shot him in the mouth. He rode on. Soon the man thought. He felt behind him and his saddle-bags with all his wealth were missing. He turned his horse about and started retracing his course. When he came to the spot where he shot his faithful dog, he looked in a clump of bushes to see if he was there. He was not. He saw, instead, a blood-stream down the road. He followed it. When he came to the bubbling spring, there was his faithful Fido with head on the saddle-bags, dead.

Dear Friend! Would you know something of the unsearchable riches of Christ and draw upon them from day to day for grace and strength to serve and honor him? Follow the blood-stream and these riches shall be yours in great abundance. Knowing, therefore, the fear of the Lord; knowing that someday we must appear before the judgment-seat, we persuade men by preaching to the lost world the unsearchable riches of Christ.

THE LAST QUESTION EVER ASKED

TEXT: No man cared for my soul.—Psalm 142: 4.

Some years ago, in Jacksonville, Florida, a police-
man served for twenty years as traffic officer. His business was to keep traffic in that great city moving, by
directing and signaling the many tourists and travelers
who passed his street intersection constantly. During
these twenty years, he was asked all sorts of questions
about all sorts of matters by the thousands who passed
that way. He was asked the direction and mileage to
thousands of places; his opinion about hundreds of
questions; about his own personal health; the welfare
of his personal family and a multitude of other things.
One day, after spending twenty years directing traffic
and being quizzed by thousands of people, one man came
and asked him if he were a Christian.

This question, asked concerning his soul's welfare by
one who cared, made him think. As he thought, his
soul was aroused and moved toward God. He confessed his Lord, followed him in baptism, and was a
faithful and loyal deacon in the great Main Street Baptist Church of that city. Yes! the last question one is
ever asked is that about his soul. No wonder David
cried out in his distress, "No man cared for my soul."

A railroad man served fifteen years as a train conductor. During this time he met thousands of people and was asked all sorts of questions about connections and schedules; the weather and a thousand and one other things. Then one man finally asked about his soul. Only one man in fifteen years seemed to care about his soul. What awful neglect! What utter indifference! David must have been burdened and broken when he said, "No man cared for my soul."

Again, a traveler who had made the trip around the globe three times and had met and conversed with thousands of people from all walks of life, mixed and mingled with those from many nations of the earth, said that during his three trips around the world only two people ever inquired of him about his soul. The world made no inquiry about his soul because the world is not interested in the souls of men. "No man cared for my soul," cried David years and years ago. Is it still true today as it was then?

Some years ago, a godly woman visited a young man in a death cell as he waited for that day and hour to come when the harness of death would be carefully placed upon him and his soul sent out into the great beyond. As this good woman tried to talk to this poor soul about his spiritual welfare, he said, "In all my life, no one ever spoke to me about my soul until I was brought to this terrible place of death. If some one had manifested an interest in my soul, perhaps I would never have been brought here."

This man did not grow up in heathen China, nor was he born in savage Africa, nor had he his being in benighted India, nor moved in priest-ridden South America, but he lived and moved and had his being in Christian America. What a terrible indictment was this man's statement against his father and mother, his teachers, his groceryman, his bankers, his neighbors, his friends, his brothers, his sister, his employers, his barbers, his doctors, his druggists, his shoeshiners, and all with whom he came in daily contact! Did David speak the truth when he said, "No man cared for my soul"? The last question one is ever asked is a question about the soul. The last concern manifested is a concern for one's soul. The last burden ever borne is the burden for souls. What careless, cold, negligent, and indifferent servants we are to our Lord who made the first and supreme passion of his life the care for souls of men everywhere!

The world has arranged to provide every care for man's body, satisfy every whim of his soul, gratify every foible of his mind, tickle every fancy of his imagination, and minister to every phase of his being except his spiritual, eternal, and everlasting welfare. That which shall never perish, that which shall never be dissolved, that which shall never cease to be, that which does not "return, dust to dust and ashes to ashes,"—that no man cares about.

I have had more than one man tell me that I was the first person that ever spoke to them about their souls. Others had spoken to them about many things, but if they cared for their souls, this care had not been manifested. I know a tailor who declared that he had measured a certain preacher time and time again for a suit of clothes, but never once, said the tailor, did the preacher inquire about his soul.

Right here sad mistakes are made by fathers and mothers with their children. They exercise abundant care for every phase of the child's welfare except the welfare of their souls. They supply them with the best food and raiment; they give them the best opportunities in school to train their minds; they secure the most skilled physicians when they are ill, paying their last farthing for medicines and nurses and hospitals;—but their souls! Oh, their immortal souls! they seem to care nothing at all about.

It has been said that the man who started the American Unitarian Movement, as a boy, heard a sermon on the "Judgment." He was greatly moved by the passionate sermon. He inquired of his father, a professed Christian and a good moral man, about the matter of the judgment, but his father seemed utterly unconcerned about the whole matter. The boy naturally had great confidence in his father. Seeing him so unconcerned about so great a matter, he decided that the preacher in his earnest effort to declare the whole counsel of God, was hair-brained. As he grew to manhood, and yearning for some sort of religious expression, he started the Unitarian Movement, teaching that Jesus was no more the Son of God than the least among men.

Oh! if that father had moved with God and had manifested some little concern about his boy's soul, he would not only have reached his boy for Jesus but would have saved America from one of its most blighting of heresies! No wonder any child is hard to reach when by indifference and neglect and unconcern, the parents manifest no care for their child's soul. Here is a problem that should stir us to action. Many times this is true in our best homes and at times in the homes of the workers of our churches. To sin here is great sin and many times results in heart-breaking consequences.

Oh! to get people to move with God as the Israelites

did in the wilderness is a great problem and, too, a great joy when they so move. I am thinking now of a maiden lady of my home community who grew up in one of the best homes of that community and while a young girl, she was moved toward God. Her parents, like scores of others, unsympathetically and unwisely, had her to suppress that interest and she failed to find God at that season. That interest in her soul died as she quenched the Spirit. In all these after years, with all the persuasion and all the urging from her parents and Christian workers, she, like Felix, has never found a convenient season. Today, she has passed the meridian of life and is still without Christ, still unconcerned, still without care for her soul. Some day I shall read of this woman's death, and if her course of life continues as it is, she will go into eternity without God. If those parents had been wise, they would have encouraged her to let that interest in her soul fructify into the acceptance of Christ Jesus as her Saviour.

There are so many reasons why we should care for the souls of men. First, the Kingdom workers have come from homes where a sympathetic interest and a sincere care for their souls were manifested. A study of the biographies of one hundred twenty-eight missionaries some years ago revealed the fact that one hundred twenty-one came from homes that were deeply and manifestly religious—homes that magnified Christ, homes that were loyal to the program of the church, faithful in the work of our Lord, and reverent in spirit; homes where it was easy in youth to find God.

My warm friend and earnest worker, Mr. W. P. Phillips, of the Baptist Sunday School Board, tells of his experience with his only son, who was then a mere lad. A series of meetings was being conducted in his church and the time, he felt, had come when his laddie should be led to the Lord. He decided that no other man should deprive him of the joy of leading his own boy to Jesus. He took the week off from his work and made it his business that week to lead his son to Jesus. He said: "One of the happiest experiences of my life was when I walked down the aisle with my boy and saw him surrender his all to the Lord." Here was a father who cared for the soul of his boy, and what a joy it was to his heart to see him come to Jesus! What a tragedy it must be for any man to look back over his life and be compelled by circumstances to say of his mother and father, "No man cared for my soul"!

A second reason for caring for the souls of men is because many men are anxious and will respond to the proper interest in their souls. Down deep in the hearts of all men there is a heart hunger for God. They may try to hide it and suppress it and conceal it; they may try to cover it with all sorts of excuses, but it is there and, like Banquo's Ghost, it will not down. They care for their souls because they know that life is uncertain. None knows when the brittle cord of life will be snapped and his soul thrust into a godless eternity. If men would think on their evil ways and on the uncertainty of life, earnestly and seriously, there would be no trouble in reaching people for God. Two weeks after a most gracious revival meeting in the First Baptist Church of Live Oak, Florida, the pastor, Rev. L. B. White, wrote saying that an old man, seventy years old, had passed away. I remembered him distinctly. He called one day at a home in which we were guests. He was laughing and joking about many things but never once did he attend any service of the series of meetings at the church. He never realized that within two short weeks, his body would be lying stiff and cold in the grave where "dust would return to dust and ashes to ashes." He failed to realize that his tongue, so ready with jokes, would in two weeks be silent in death; that his fingers, so nimble to be so old, would be cold and stiff; that his eyes, so sparkling with humor, would soon lose their luster; and the mind so active, would be tormented with remorse and regret.

But some one might say that this man had reached the limit of life and death must be expected at his age. But life even in youth is also uncertain. A short time ago, a good woman, who had some young men rooming in her home, said that one day she had a very frank and serious talk with one of them. She urged upon him the importance of accepting Christ, of being ready to meet God. He put this good woman off by saying that since he was young and in the very heyday of life, he had plenty of time to think about his soul. But did he? Oh! did he have plenty of time? The world said he did. Satan persuaded him that he did. Biology said that he did. Statistics said that he probably did. But in a few brief months, as he and some friends were driving on the slippery pavement of a nearby city, one Sunday afternoon while out joy-riding, his car skidded and went into a telephone pole and his soul was hurled into eternity, unprepared to meet his God. David, while pursued by Saul, declared: "There is but a step between me and death." That step is growing shorter as civilization becomes more complex. Life, more now than ever, is most uncertain, and this fact should influence men to care for their souls.

Another reason is because of the reality of God's saving grace. Christ Jesus, God's only begotten and beloved Son, can change the hearts of men. He saves with an everlasting salvation. He turns men about and starts them on the road to right living. He effects a transformation in their lives. It makes a great deal of difference when one comes to die whether he has made it right with God or not. There is reality in the saving power of Jesus.

Some years ago, at the world's fair in Chicago, there was a parliament of religions. Every religious faith and sect were represented. The priest of Buddha with his long flowing robe; the representative of Mohammedanism with his towering fez; the spokesman for Confucianism with his pigtail queue,—all were there to declare the excellencies of their rites and rituals, of their forms and faiths. They were seated in a semicircle. The time came for the representative of Christianity to speak. He arose and greeted all in the name of Jesus. In his address he described graphically and vividly the scene of Lady Macbeth, sleepless and nervous after the murder of King Duncan. The murder was upon her soul, and as she walked the floor of her bedroom, dressed in her silks, she spoke to that bloody spot on her hand and cried: "Out, damned spot! out, I say! . . . All the perfumes of Arabia will not sweeten this little hand." Then this great Christian preacher turned to the representatives of the religions of the world and asked: "Gentlemen! have you anything that will cleanse that woman's hand?" They shook their heads and declared that they did not. Then turning to his audience he said: "Thank God, we have, for the blood of Jesus Christ his Son cleanseth us from all sin." When we realize that it does matter whether one is saved or not, we will care mightily for the souls of men everywhere. God save the preachers and workers from professionalism! God save us from the familiarity which breeds neglect and indifference! God save us from ever thinking that it does not matter whether one is right with God or not!

Again, we should have a care for the souls of men because of the impressions made on us in early youth by those who have asked about *our* souls. These are the impressions that last down through life's long day. These are the ones that are imperishable. These are they that never fade away. Some of you can feel yet the hand that rested on your head and hear yet the appealing voice that spoke about your soul long years ago. A traveler, vitally interested in the life of the great Scotch preacher, Robert McCheyne, visited the community in which he had ministered. He was anxious to find some one who had seen and heard the great preacher. He met an old man who as a boy remembered the old preacher. As the old man told of the impressions the great preacher made upon his soul, he said: "One day, I remember, he came to visit my sister who was dying. As he talked, he placed his loving hand on my head. I can feel the touch of that hand yet, and still hear his voice as he urged me, saying, 'My boy, give your heart to Jesus.' Sir! in all my long life, I have never gotten away from those words nor from the loving touch of that hand." The old man remembered the great preacher because he cared for his soul.

John G. Paton, that marvelous missionary to the New Hebrides, tells in his life story of his father who, every night as he approached the throne of grace in his family

worship, remembered in his earnest prayer the lost. One
night as he prayed, an outcast woman crouched at his
window and heard him pray for her soul. Her heart
was moved mightily by the sincere, earnest prayer of the
man of God. She arose and left behind her the old life
and turned to God, because somebody cared for her lost
and undone soul.

The one supreme care of every child of God should
be an interest, an abiding, everlasting interest, a heart-
hungering interest, a soul-longing interest in the spiritual welfare of man. No preacher can give to every
member of his church a job. I once heard of a preacher
who had set up such an organization in his church that
every member had some particular task to perform. I
never heard afterwards one word from this great mass
of machinery. Such an organization would be too
clumsy for service and too awkward for efficiency. If
we are saved, if we are alive and interested in the on-
going of the church, we will not wait until the preacher
or some church official assigns to us a task; we will go
out and seek others for Jesus.

It is said that an engineer came to Mr. Spurgeon
and asked him for something to do in his church. The
preacher looked him in the eye and asked: "Is your
fireman a Christian?" The engineer replied that he
was not. "Then that is *your* job until you win *him*
to Jesus," said the preacher.

There are a thousand ways to show your care for the
souls of men. The spoken word, the labor of love, some
kindness manifested, moving your church membership,
attendance on the worship of God, earnest prayer in
their behalf, and loyalty to the services of your church.
Some years ago there came into our church with her

membership, a mother. That night her daughter came for baptism. The father was spoken to and he was interested, and the son was moved toward God. This wife manifested her care by moving her church membership. The daughter and husband and son saw that the mother and wife had more than a passing interest and they were moved, too, to God. Surely you will not give the dearest and nearest to your heart occasion to say, "No man cared for my soul."

We should care for the souls of men because Jesus Christ and him crucified is the world's only hope. The world is sick and feverish and restless and tossing. There are many remedies prescribed for the world's ills. The teacher says that more knowledge is the remedy, but we know now better than we do. The artists say that more beauty is the remedy, but a bouquet of flowers will not ease the cutting pains of blood poison. The philosopher says we need a new theory of life, but we do not now live perfectly the theories we have. The supreme need of the world is Jesus. He will cure every ill of every individual, of every home, of every community anywhere. He will cool the fever of the restless world, soothe its nerves, bring order out of chaos, and peace to the troubled soul. He, and he alone, is the remedy for the world's ills. Let us pour the healing balm of his grace in every open sore, and it will heal immediately and perfectly. Let us make this question, not the last ever asked but the first and foremost, and God will bless richly and abundantly.

THE POWER OF WOMANHOOD

TEXT: O woman, great is thy faith.—Matthew 15: 28.

What a marvelous blessing is a mother! A mother is the greatest institution on earth. No other institution, man-made, has ever been able to take adequately her place. Some one has said that God could not be everywhere; therefore, he made mothers. Another has said: "The hand that rocks the cradle is the hand that rules the world." It was Napoleon who said, "The thing France needs most is mothers." The greatest honor God ever bestowed on any human being was that which he bestowed on Mary, the carpenter's betrothed bride, when he trusted his only begotten Son into her care and keeping. It is no great surprise that some make much of Mary—indeed far too much—in their worship. The tender, devoted mother of our Lord has deserved more honor than many have given her. She should be elevated, but certainly not above him who is above all. All motherhood has been made sacred, beautiful, and sweet because of its importance and opportunities.

What wonder in a mother's love! What sight on this earth is more wonderful than a mother's love pouring itself into the face of a tiny, helpless babe nestled in her loving arms? But there are mothers and mothers. There are many motherless children,—far too many motherless children for any woman to pour her heart's affection on anything else other than a child. There are childless mothers. One may never have had the joy of hugging her own child in the flesh to her breast, but if she has a brooding spirit and a heart hunger for children, she is as much a mother, and many times more so than others who have been privileged to bear children. Mother-love is not conditioned by time, place, nor circumstances, but is found wherever the heart hungers for a child.

Some children have a mammy but no mother. Sam Jones used to tell of a little girl who came to her mother and said: "Mother, will you give me some scraps to make my doll a dress?" The mother answered, "I won't do it. You waste more scraps than you are worth. Now get out and quit bothering me." The little girl went out with her head dropped and murmured, "I wish I were dead. Mama never has a kind word for me." She came again another day and begged: "Mother, may I have a needle and thread to sew with?" "There you are again, you little vixen! I wish you would take your things over to Mrs. Brown's and see if you can bother her a while." The little girl walked out with her heart crushed and whispered, "I wish Mother was dead; she never seems to care for me." But she came back again and said: "Mama, lend me your thimble and scissors." "There you are again. You took my thimble the other day and I was two hours finding it. Let me catch you at that again and I'll make you dance a jig. You just want my scissors to punch your eyes out and be here on me the rest of your life blind. Now get your things and get out of here." The little girl walked out again—this time with a scowl on her face—and said: "I wish I was Mrs. Brown's little girl. Mama is just as mean to me as she can be." She went out in life and became the talk of the community. The mother grieved over her conduct and sighed, saying, "The Lord knows I've done the best I could. I don't know what's the matter with her."

The trouble was, she was just like her Mammy—a chip off the old block, plus. She needed a mother more than she needed anything else in all this world. She was endured, not endeared.

But here is a real mother busy at her tasks. Her little girl comes in and says, "Mother, I want to make my dolly a dress. Have you any scraps that I may use?" The mother smiles and says, "Yes, dear, just a moment. Mother is awfully busy today, trying to get you a new dress ready for Sunday." After a bit she received her scraps, and as she goes out with a smile playing on her face and dimples in her cheeks, she whispers, "Dolly, we have the bestest mother in the world." She comes again another day and asks for the thimble, needle, and thread. The mother turns from her work and says, "I was just thinking of you, Dear, and one great desire of mother's heart is to see you become a Christian. Will you listen while Mother reads a bit of scripture?" She reads, "Remember now thy creator in the days of thy youth." "This means, my Darling," she explains, "that you must give your little heart to God early in life that all life may be happy." The little girl goes out with a song in her soul. She comes back another day with her girlish requests. The mother patiently listens and then says, "My Dear! Mother wants to pray with you and ask God to make you a good little girl." They kneel to pray. It is said that the angels crowd around and catch a tear that slips from the soft velvet cheek as it drops out of the eyes sky-blue and they bear it up to the throne and say, "Here is the tear of a little girl whose mother is preparing her for this bright world." This little girl grows up and goes out in life with a glow of love and heaven on her face. She becomes a woman, intelligent, beautiful, winsome, and pure as the drifted snow. Give the world good mothers and we need not be anxious about the daughters. What a blessing is a godly mother to a beloved daughter!

Let us consider a bit the mother who came to Jesus in behalf of her daughter. Jesus tried to hide himself as he withdrew to the coasts of Tyre and Sidon. But Jesus has never been able successfully to hide himself. When he was born the angels announced his birth to the shepherds watching at night over their flocks on the Judean hills. The Star of Bethlehem guided the wise men from the East to the country of his birth. The Scriptures revealed the little town in which he was to be born. The Holy Spirit revealed his presence to the hearts of Simeon and Anna when he was presented, forty days old, to the Lord in the Temple. You couldn't hide Jesus then. You can't hide Jesus now. If he is in your heart, he will reveal himself through your hands and feet, by the tone of your voice, by the words of your lips, and in the glow on your face. But who wants to hide Jesus?

This mother who came to Jesus, with all a mother's love and anxiety, learned that he had come into her territory. Surely she had heard how he had cured, healed, and saved others. Her daughter was grievously vexed with a demon. The most hopeful thing of all was that this mother realized her daughter's condition.

We do not know how this demon manifested itself, whether by lying, by disobedience, by pride, or by fits and spells. Demons have always manifested themselves in various ways.

Two things we know about this mother's daughter: she was little and was possessed with an unclean spirit. How large must your daughter become before she ceases to be little? A mother asked my friend who called at her home one day if he had seen her "baby." He replied that he had not. So she left the room to get her "baby," and he expected her to bring in a tiny thing on a pillar, but when she returned to the room she introduced a woman that looked as if she might weigh two hundred pounds. And still she was her baby. This Canaanitish mother's daughter must have been between the ages of ten and eighteen. If the unclean spirit develops, it will develop between these ages. If mothers can get their daughters over fool's hill, they are fairly safe; but watch for the unclean spirit between the ages of ten and eighteen.

Again, it is said that she possessed an unclean spirit. Scriptural language is not strange nor uncommon language. An unclean spirit is an ugly, dirty, foul, and wicked spirit. We speak of the spirit of a person being attractive or repulsive; winsome or wicked; beautiful or ugly; good or bad. Mark's Gospel says that this girl's spirit was "unclean." So let me name for you some unclean spirits that possess our daughters today.

The spirit of disobedience is an unclean spirit. If you tell your daughter to come back and she goes on, the spirit of disobedience possesses her. Does she come in from her dates at the hour you set? Is she guided by your counsel? What trouble, tragedy, and sorrow come because of the spirit of disobedience! I am thinking now of a young woman who called me up in a hotel in West Palm Beach, Florida, some years ago because she saw my name on the hotel register. When she called my room phone I asked who she was. Her reply was that she was Mrs. A's daughter. I asked, "Miss Mary?" "No!" she said, "the other one." I said, "Oh! what are you doing down here?" She replied, "I am down here nursing." I knew that girl. She came from a fine family. I knew her story. The first wrong step she took was one night when she disobeyed her mother. From that act of disobedience sore trouble came. A life was ruined. A name was tarnished and disgraced. Hearts were broken and grief was sore. God forbid the thought that passed through my mind when she called me in that hotel! Could it be that she had thrown herself away and had sunk so low that she was in that great winter resort working the hotels? The spirit of disobedience is an unclean, unholy, and ugly spirit. Beware of it!

The spirit of *lying* is another unclean spirit which possesses our girls and vexes them grievously. The girl who deliberately lies to her mother and practices deception takes her first step toward hell. Oh! you daughters, never let this unclean spirit of deception enter your heart! Be honest, sincere, and frank with that mother whatever else you may or may not do. I would unbosom all to her.

I am thinking of another girl who told her mother that she was going to a Sunday school class party. She went and stayed ten minutes and spent the rest of the evening in a dance hall. She deliberately deceived her mother. What a wicked, foul spirit is that of lying!

It is begotten in hell and comes fresh from the incubator of wickedness and enters your daughter's heart. Pray that God may save your daughter from such a spirit!

What a responsibility is that of a mother! Don't leave your daughters to choose their own way in this world. What terrible conduct is found in the roadhouses and dance halls of today by girls who are left to choose their own way! It is a shame ever to speak of. Commander Margaret Bevil of the Salvation Army said, some years ago, that forty-two per cent of the unmarried mothers in fifteen maternity homes had been schoolgirls of high or elementary grades, averaging sixteen years of age. The majority of the girls attribute their trouble to late automobile rides. Twenty years ago, these homes were filled with women of mature age, but now they go from the schoolroom. The age of love-making and dates is dropping and girls not much more than overgrown babies have evening dresses and entertain with elaborate parties. It ought not so to be.

Late hours with dates are not conducive to good morals. Our daughters ought to be taught to keep decent hours with their dates. Some years ago, while conducting a series of meetings, I was a guest in a hotel that served for a teacherage. Returning one evening from a church service, I saw a young woman dressed as if she had been to the preaching service. I asked her if she attended the service at the church that evening. She smiled and said, "No, I am waiting for my date." It was then ten o'clock in the evening. Soon a young man drove up and, picking her up, they started out. I said, "Surely, things have changed!" When I did my courting, this was the time I used to leave.

But now it is the time when they begin, and when they get in, I don't know, for I seldom stay up so late. But this change is not for the best interests of our young people.

We ought to provide a room in our homes where our daughters may receive their friends privately. These necking and petting parties in parked automobiles are a result largely of our failure to provide adequately in our homes for our young people. In the great and many changes taking place, one institution that has passed is that of the old-fashioned parlor. Here is where the daughter of yesterday received her friends. We lost mightily when we cut out of our homes the old-fashioned parlor. If we would keep our young people from the highways, let us provide a place for them in our homes.

The desire of every true mother's heart is to see her daughter popular with the right sort of young man. Most of us who have daughters would be delighted to see a fine young man of character park his car in front of our home. Let us train these daughters in right living, and they will have the right sort of popularity. There are three kinds of popularity: the peacock, the monkey, and that which comes from what one is and can do. The peacock popularity is that which attracts by dress and looks. This popularity is transient. The monkey popularity is that which comes from capers cut and dances indulged. This popularity is also passing. But the popularity which comes from what one is and can do, is the popularity that lasts and endures. I would like for a daughter of mine to be able to paint a picture, sing a song, play a piece of music, cook and serve a good meal's victuals, sweep a room clean, and above all, know how to keep house and make a home.

I believe in the old-fashioned girl from which the old-fashioned mother came,—a girl who can boil a pot of water without scorching it; who can cook a biscuit that won't sink when dropped in water; who can darn a sock that won't rub all the skin off the heel; who can sew on a patch so cleverly that it can't be detected a block away. There is today entirely too much drug-store complexion and far too little home connection. In our supply of good lookers, we have failed to produce a supply of good cookers. Many a man thought he was getting a good cook and found out later that all he got was a can opener. You can get one of them in any dime store. The popularity that endures and lasts comes from what one is and can do. In choosing a wife, character and accomplishment should count far more than proficiency in dancing and profusion in dress and jewels.

Consider the power of women to mold and shape the moral and religious life of man. The devil knows the wonderful power of woman. When he desires to accomplish some rotten piece of work, he chooses many times a woman and works through her. When he sought to destroy the perfect joy of Eden, he went to the woman first. He knew if he got Eve, he would get Adam before the sun went down. And he did. When he sought to shear the locks from the head of the mighty Samson, he induced him to lay that head in Delilah's lap. And the locks came off. When he tried to get the courageous Elijah on the run, he got Jezebel in behind him and Elijah ran like a marathon runner! No *man* could intimidate Simon Peter. Was he not courageous enough to cut off the ear of the high priest's servant? But when a little maid pointed her accusing finger as he warmed by the enemy's fire, he cursed and swore like an old-timer.

Business has learned the attractiveness of woman, and a beautiful young woman is used to advertise nearly every commodity on sale except "Brown Mule Tobacco." This stands on its own merits. Somebody has said that good advertising is the picture of a young woman drinking, smelling, tasting, smoking, wearing, riding, or thrilling over some commodity for sale. The devil never gained a greater victory than when he put a cigaret in the hands of a beautiful young woman to advertise it. The business world has never before exploited to such a tremendous and degrading extent the power and influence of women as it is doing today. May God help our women to use their great influence for the things that are true, things that are good, things that are beautiful, and things that are right.

If the devil has used women in his work of corruption, God has also used them and mightily blessed them. There is only one good woman mentioned in the Bible who did not have a fairly decent husband—Abigail. Her husband's name was Nabal. This name Nabal means "fool." If a woman is married to a fool, she may as well give up trying to reach him for Christ. The influence of a wife over her husband is greater than that of any other influence, moral or religious, that comes into his life. The Bible sustains me in this statement. God says that Ahab was the most wicked king that ever sat on the throne *because of Jezebel, his wife;* that Solomon's heart was stolen from him in his later years because of his wives, some of whom came out of Egypt. Haman's wife urged him on in his wickedness, and she later looked on him dangling from the gallows he made for Mordecai. Sapphira was privy to the plans of Ananias to lie to the Holy Spirit about their gift to the church, and evidently she encouraged him in this great sin of attempted deception. Any woman who encourages her husband in wickedness is courting death. I always tremble when I find a wife and mother without God in her home. Many times it means that that home is wholly without religious influence.

So great is the power of a wife over her husband that she usually can make out of him anything she wants him to be religiously or morally. If your husband goes to hell, it is because you don't care enough. I asked a certain man if this statement were true, and he replied, "Yes, it is literally true. When I married my wife, I was not a Christian, but so faithful and true to Christ was she that I soon found out if I lived with her I had to be a Christian." That man is a deacon in a prominent Baptist church. Sam Houston's Margaret Lee took a wild boar and won him to Christ. She molded him into a great husband. The last words of this great character were the two greatest influences in his life—"Margaret, Margaret, Texas, Texas." These were the two supreme forces that came into his great soul. Time would fail me and space would forbid giving the many illustrations of great, strong, Christian men who have been won to the Lord by their devoted and faithful Christian wives.

King Solomon knew the prestige of woman when he made her the queen of the chess-board. She is the most powerful fighter in the game and ablest defender of the king. Woman makes the home, rears the children, and keeps man from being a brute. Woman will curse us or bless us. She will drag us down to the pits of hell or lift us up to the gates of glory. She will inspire us to do our best or nag and tempt us to do our worst. Thank God for the influence and power of a Christian woman!

What mighty influence woman has wielded in the fight against liquor. She gave our nation prohibition, and if it ever comes back she must lead in the fight. I shall never forget when a boy hearing a young woman give that recitation, "The lips that touch liquor shall never touch mine." If our wives and sweethearts would make this sentiment their motto, it would do more to bring an end to humanity's greatest curse than anything that could be done. If a man loved his bottle better than he did me, I would tell him to take it and go to the dogs, where he will end finally. I wouldn't want a daughter of mine to marry a lounge lizard with a liquor bottle tied to his neck.

What mighty blessings earth has received from the prayers of godly women! This Canaanitish woman was a praying mother. She was one of great faith. Jesus said, "O woman, great is thy faith: be it unto thee even as thou wilt." I would like to see one newspaper edited by Jesus,—how he would write up the victories gained and the great faith of his people and the great good resulting from their prayers.

The little prayer that mothers used to teach to their children has been a stay to many a soul, years later as trouble and sorrow and death came. I knew a man seventy years of age, who had lost most of his material wealth. He developed heart trouble and was unable for weeks to lie down. At times he was reasonable and rational and at other times his mind wandered. The end of the way came. His children sat in the room with him one Sunday evening. They said, "Father, it's time now to go to bed!" He said, "Yes! but before we go, let's pray." And I think his mind must have wandered and he thought himself a boy again at his mother's knee. So, he folded his old wrinkled hands and with an upturned face, he said:

> Now, I lay me down to sleep,
> I pray Thee, Lord, my soul to keep;
> If I should die before I wake,
> I pray Thee, Lord, my soul to take.
> This I ask for Jesus' sake. Amen.

Then he leaned over on his pillows and in a few minutes he was fast asleep. The family waited and in a few minutes more they heard the death rattle, and saw him become limp in death. As they rushed to his side, he was gone. In the very hour and article of death, the mother's prayer she had taught her boy became a stay to his soul.

There is no place in all the world that is nearer heaven than at a mother's knee. Some years ago, a mother, busy at her work, said to her two boys, "You must say your prayers now and go to bed." They came and said, "Mother, we want to say our prayers at your knee." She laid aside her work and went in to the bedroom and with one boy at one knee and the other at the other knee, with a hand of blessing on each tousled head, they said their prayers. Then, she kissed them good-night. What a blessing! What a privilege for such children! But a next-door neighbor's children about the same age had to go to bed that same night without a mother's kiss and without a mother's benediction.

O mothers, in your struggle for righteousness, I beg you never to give up! Your prayers have stood between many a man and hell. The memories of a godly mother, like merciful angels, have come often and delivered many a soul from the city of destruction. Put into the soul of your daughters the love of God and the fear of sin; teach your sons the way to God and throw around your husband an influence that grips and lifts, and Jesus will say again, as he did of old, "O woman, great is thy faith: be it unto thee even as thou wilt." And the deep down desires of your heart shall be yours in the greatest of fulness as the years come and go. Don't give up and quit. Keep on keeping on for God and home!

CIVIC RIGHTEOUSNESS

(Delivered at Baptist State Convention of Texas, Mineral Wells, in November, 1936.)

TEXT: Righteousness exalteth a nation: but sin is a reproach to any people.—Proverbs 14: 34.

> Standing beside the highway of life,
>   Watching the world go by,—
> Men who are good and men who are bad,
>   As good and as bad as you and I.

We ask seriously and solemnly the same question that was asked the fleeing apostle from Rome, "Quo Vadis?" "Whither goest thou?" Where are we headed—to the jungle or to Jerusalem? What will be the end of the way—the valley of Achor or the uplands of God?

No reasonable and sane man can seriously contemplate the signs of the times and not be upset and disturbed by many of these signs. I am not a pessimist nor the son of a pessimist, but there are many things about us and among us which are disturbing and many other things that should give us great cause and ground for rejoicing. Some are alarmed about our young people. But they are no worse than we "when you and I were young, Maggie." I have the utmost confidence in any young man or woman who has been trained properly. I have absolutely no confidence in any young man or woman who has not been trained properly. If there is a breakdown in morals among our young people, the break came before this generation of young people came on the stage.

Some are much alarmed over the condition existing in our nation, but if conditions here are alarming, it is because of the breakdown in our homes. No river can rise higher than its source, and no nation can rise higher than its homes. As a river reflects the nature of its head waters, so a nation reflects the spirit of its homes.

What are some of the disturbing facts? One is the desecration of the Lord's Day. We have traveled far in the wrong direction from the pioneer pilgrim on his way to church, as he carried his flintrock rifle for protection from Indians, walking by the side of his demure wife with her Bible and modest dress, to the man today, with his family in a speeding automobile, spending the week-end in pursuit of pleasure, business, or dissipation.

The devil has made no greater attack on any Christian institution of today than on that of the Lord's Day. The popular and recently introduced Saturday night dance is as much an attack on the Lord's Day as the opening of the movies on Sunday. Sunday school attendants and church worshipers do not come from the Saturday night dance. We are witnessing the tragic transformation of Sunday into a fun day, of the Holy day into a holiday, of the Lord's Day changed to the devil's day. It is no longer now the Sabbath, or Lord's Day, or Sunday, but the "week-end," and it may be spelled "week" or "weak." The question now is, "What will you do with the week-end?"

The desecration of the Lord's Day is a direct result

of a mad pleasure craze which has gripped the public. The church, if it survives, must have a day in which men and women give themselves to prayer, to the study of God's Word, to worship, to praise and meditation. The Lord's Day is a river whose streams make glad the city of God and if we fail to bathe our souls in this stream, we fail tragically in the highest and best of this world. Righteousness must have a day of spiritual re-enforcement and moral strengthening, or we lose our moral standards of right and wrong. We will be guilty of the blinding sin of calling good evil, and evil good, of putting light for darkness, and darkness for light; our moral sense so vitiated that we shall call bitter sweet, and sweet bitter.

Another alarming fact is the breakdown of the home. The rate of increase in divorces today is most alarming. If Christ built his church on divine revelation and regeneration, a civilization to be secure must be built on homes of happiness, trust, and mutual confidence. In one great city of Texas, it is said that three out of every five marriages contracted prove to be a failure.

It is believed that much of the seed of discord destroying the mutual confidence and trust in the home is sown in the ballroom and dance hall. Here, where the bodies of men and women are brought in such close proximity and where the ties that bind a man and his wife are so strained, is the beginning of the tragic end of many marriages. Here, where the passions are inflamed, is the sowing of the seed that ripens into the harvest of heartaches, disrupted homes, and separated families.

Some one has said of all the inmates of penal and reform institutions none has been found who came from happy homes. Another has said that two signs of a decadent civilization are the breakdown of the home and kidnapping. Surely we have had enough of both to be alarmed over.

Another fearful fact is the strong drink problem. Liquor is back with us in legal standing and in full force. None of the fair promises of the wets has been fulfilled. One encouraging sign is that the breweries and liquor manufacturers are becoming disturbed over the great debacle we have been plunged into.

God said long ago that "wine is a mocker and strong drink is raging." That statement is as up-to-date as if it were written yesterday. Medical science has proved beyond a shadow of a doubt that alcoholic liquors constitute a narcotic poison, the effect of which on the body is to produce, among many other evils, carelessness. The last thing we need in this day of high speed and delicate mechanism is carelessness. If there were such a drug that would make men cautious and careful, I know many who ought to be compelled to take a pint three times a day. One who is intoxicated is poisoned, and such are to be pitied above all men. We would never think of poisoning our pigs, but many have no conscientious scruples against voting to poison our boys and girls.

The ultimate result of strong drink is crime. For crime and drink have always risen in parallel lines on the statistician's scale of averages. We need again the swing of Carry Nation's hatchet to catch the public fancy and let the sound of that hatchet echo across the land. We need more recitations on "the lips that touch liquor shall never touch mine." We need to crystallize public sentiment:

Against this terrible weight that hobbles every drink addict.

Against this awful habit that degrades all who form it.

Against this mocker that makes fools of all who come under its influence.

Against this hydra-headed monster that poisons all who play with it.

Against this foul fountain that can never be purified.

Against this reptile that bites like a serpent and stings like an adder.

Liquor taxation is always the recourse of bankrupt statesmanship, when poverty-stricken politicians try to meet the expenses of a spendthrift government. A nation has never yet drunk its way to prosperity. It is in direct conflict with all the laws of economy. The garbage man in our great cities has sensed the situation and cries, "Bottles and rags, bottles and rags." He has learned by experience that where he finds bottles, he will sooner or later find rags, too. All the great and good of all the ages are against this greatest and most unbearable burden of the poor and unspeakable curse of the rich. As some one has said, the liquor traffic from A to Z is that it:

> Arms more villains
> Breaks more laws
> Corrupts more officials
> Destroys more homes
> Engulfs more fortunes
> Fills more jails
> Grows more gray hairs
> Harrows more hearts
> Incites more crime

Jeopardizes more lives
Kindles more strife
Lacerates more feelings
Maims more bodies
Nails down more coffins
Opens more graves
Poisons more minds
Quenches more songs
Raises more sobs
Sells more virtue
Tells more lies
Undermines more youth
Violates more decencies
Wrecks more men
Xcites more murders
Yields more disgrace
Zeroes more hopes

than any enemy of mankind. The druggist's "cross-bones and skull"—the emblem of poison—ought to be printed in bold relief upon every liquor bottle ever filled with this poison.

If the picture is dark and gloomy as we look upon the evils of the age, there is another picture which gives hope and begets courage. If crimes cost the American people annually, as statistics prove, fifteen billion dollars and 3,500,000 are involved in the commission of 1,500,000 major crimes annually, and if every forty-five minutes mark the death in America of some one by violence, as stated by authority, we have weapons which are not carnal but mighty through God unto the casting down of strongholds.

The first steps we must climb toward a spiritual awakening and moral recovery are the church steps.

There is a decided tendency toward the church. Mr. Henry C. Link, a noted psychologist, has written a book on *My Return to Religion,* confessing the futility of education without the spiritual and moral content. The church must take its place and will find its place finally along with the college and university and institutions of learning. Science has been busy elaborating, multiplying, and expanding the means of living. The church must give to man the great purpose of living. Those whose lives are marked with spiritual idiocy and moral lunacy must realize that life is tragic without spiritual wisdom and moral understanding.

The first stand we must take is the pulpit stand. The preached Word of God is a power for civic righteousness which has never yet been equaled by any other means. When Paul entered the city of seven hills as a gospel preacher—a prisoner of Rome—there came the greatest force for righteousness that ever passed into the city of seven hills. Cæsar crossing the Rubicon in ultimate consequences was nothing to be compared to Paul coming with the gospel of Christ.

And what mighty transformation this mighty gospel leaven of the great missionary brought about in the Roman Empire! Rome's polytheism gave way before the doctrine of monotheism. Christianity preached that there is one holy, just, righteous, and merciful God. So mighty was this power of God that Paul was not ashamed of it, that in 313 the Emperor Constantine of the great empire accepted Christianity as his faith. Christianity with its doctrine of one God, holy and righteous, triumphed over the doctrine of many gods with no moral significance and rose from a sect, despised and persecuted, to a place of supreme importance in the greatest empire of the world in less than three hundred fifty years.

Christianity found slavery in the Roman Empire in its most horrible form—sixty million slaves, there were —and by teaching and preaching the brotherhood of man, mitigated the horrors and finally struck the shackles from every Roman slave.

Christianity found the gory gladiatorial shows, the most brutal and cruel sport of the human race. In 404 the gladiatorial contests were abolished by law. Lecky, the faithful historian, says, "There is scarcely any other single reform in the moral history of mankind so important as the suppression of the gladiatorial shows, and this feat must be almost exclusively ascribed to the Christian church."

We claim to live in an age of great wealth; but the question is, did riches get us, or did we get riches? Do our possessions possess us, or do we possess them? Have they become our master, or have we made them our servant? A fortune placed in ungodly and untried hands is the greatest curse that might befall any one. We must learn to give as well as get, or we are undone.

We claim to live in an age of reason. It is an age of popular education. It is an age of crowded colleges and universities; yet one pistol shot in 1914 set the world on fire. Educate a fool and all you have is an educated fool. Educate a crook and you multiply his power for crookedness by tens and twenties. Culture and consecration are the greatest combination I have ever seen in any soul. Culture without consecration is tragic beyond words. Consecration without culture results in a lopsided fanatic. I am persuaded that the ups and outs cause more hell among us than the downs and outs. We need a revival to begin at the top rung of society and work to the very bottom rung of human existence.

Do we have evils today? Yes! we are in the trough of a wave of immorality, crime and drink and gambling, but we have the same gospel which is still the power of God. We have the same Christ who still has all authority given unto him. We have the same Holy Spirit, who is ready to clothe us with power from on high and warm our hearts with the flame and cleanse our souls from all unrighteousness. We have the same gracious unbroken promise of his presence unto the end of the world. We serve the same God, who is mightier than the devil and who caused the walls of wicked Jericho to crumble, who fed Elijah with the ravens at Cherith, who opened the prison doors for Peter, and who brought again from the dead, Jesus Christ. Let us preach it, live it, teach it, and propagate it and the victory will be ours! The panacea and one remedy is Jesus—Jesus only.

Last of all, righteousness, not regal splendor, not power, not culture, not wealth, but righteousness exalteth a nation.

THE FATHER IN BEHALF OF HIS SON

TEXT: Lord, have mercy on my son.—Matthew 17 : 15.

The greatest thought we have about God is "Father-hood." Jesus said, "When you pray, say, 'Our Father who art in heaven.'" The greatest character in all human history is known as the "Son"—"Son of man and Son of God." "The Son of man came not to be ministered unto, but to minister, and to give his life a ransom for many." The highest ideal and greatest desire of a son is so to live that his life will be well pleasing to a righteous father. It was said of Jesus, "This is my beloved Son, in whom I am well pleased." "The fatherhood of God" and "The sonship of Jesus Christ" are written in golden letters throughout the New Testament.

Fatherhood carries with it mighty responsibility. God's ideal of a father is that of priest of his household. The Hebrew father was the one who must lead his household religiously and teach his children the things of God. He was primarily the one to stand between God and his family. It takes no prophet to see that we, as fathers today, have failed sorely at this point. In the great majority of homes, if the children are taught religiously, the mother must do it. But that duty, my brother, God expects of us and not of our wives. If our children had to wait until we taught them about God, many would never learn. They would grow up as ignorant of God as a rank savage in Africa. That responsibility is ours! It is not only a responsibility but it is a high privilege and a marvelous opportunity. Let us assume it.

In our bestowal of honor and praise, we have too often slightly slighted father. He has never received the credit which many have so richly deserved. Mother has received pæons of glory and honor, and she richly deserves all that we can bestow. But father deserves more recognition and more of our praise. His work is of such a prosaic nature that it does not appeal to the romantic thinker. Thus poets, speakers, and writers have failed to glorify him as they have mother. There are poems galore and songs in abundance about mother, but who has ever heard a great song about dad?

Father has been the butt of many jokes which have been told on the family. Many times he has been the goat. A pastor was once visiting among his people and called at a home where little Willie was sent out by his mother to entertain him while she was getting ready. As they talked, Willie said, "Everybody in our house is some sort of an animal." The preacher, astonished, said, "Why, Willie, you must not say that. It can't be true." "Yes!" he replied, "but it is true. It is like this. Mother is a 'dear,' baby is mother's 'little lamb,' I am the 'kid,' and dad is the 'goat.'"

Dad is not only the goat, but he is the "finicky" person, the one with such good manners (?). But however poor his manners, dad is the taxpayer, the breadwinner, the burden-bearer, and the provider. Any man who rears a family, pays the bills, puts shoes on their feet, clothes on their backs, food on the table, and educates and sends out into the world a family of boys and girls that will bless and lift the world closer to God, has made a great success if he hasn't a single cent when the transaction's done.

A father of a large family came some years ago to the writer and said, "Preacher, I'm a failure." "Why do you say so?" asked the preacher. "Because," he said, "I haven't accumulated any material wealth." The preacher replied, "But you have been a wonderful success. Any man who, like you, has reared a big family, paid their bills, provided things necessary for their material comfort, and sent them out to bless the world, has made the greatest sort of success possible if there's nothing left after it is all done." I thank God for every father who bears the financial burdens of a family.

I have the utmost respect for any man who bears the burdens of a home and family and provides for them the necessities of life. But that man who becomes a consumer instead of a provider, who wastes the living made instead of making the living, who becomes a curse instead of a blessing to his family, and a weight instead of wings—such a man deserves the contempt and scorn of all society. The shoulders that should bear the financial burdens of a family and the hands that should provide for the home are dad's.

Some men are always growling. Why a father should pour out on his family the pent-up ill feelings of the day is more than I can understand. A young wife said to her husband, "You promised before we were married to be humbly grateful, but you have proved yourself to be grumbly hateful." A wife had moved into her new home and a neighbor had come to visit, and as they went over the beautiful new home, the owner said, "This is my husband's den. Do you have a den for your husband?" "No," the neighbor replied, "my husband growls all over the house." Surely if we must growl, we will find some more fitting place to do it than in the home. The home should be the vestibule of heaven where we reveal the best that is within us.

FATHERS AND SONS. What a vital relationship! How much would you take for your father? What are you doing to fill his life full of gladness and joy? God said of John the Baptist that he would bring joy and gladness to the heart of his father. If the truth were known, it would have to be said at the birth of many sons, "He will bring sorrow and distress to his father's heart." And what terrible sorrow a son can bring to a father's heart! No grief is greater! What a source of joy other sons have become!

And your sons! What would you fathers take for them? There isn't enough wealth in the East Texas oil field to buy that boy's little finger. What are you doing to make that boy a better boy—a boy whose life will be manly and whose character will be strong? How much time are you giving to develop him into the man you would have him be? A strange gift was made one Christmas season by a big, busy, business man to his son. He was telling his neighbor about it. It was this: He placed a little note in his son's Christmas sock, saying, "My boy! I will give you this next year one hour of my time every day and three hours every Sunday." The neighbor replied, saying, "Sir, you have given your boy the greatest gift you can make—you've given him yourself." Oh! how our boys need us! A father used to come home from the city and was greeted by his small boy, saying, "Daddy, what did you bring me?" The father teasingly replied, "My son, I brought you myself." The boy replied, "Ah! pshaw—why didn't you bring me *something?*" That father brought his son the greatest gift he could bring—himself. Give your boy yourself plus God and all will be well with you and with him. This is one of the most vital points of living and one of the most far-reaching relationships. Fail here in your son and life becomes a failure everywhere. Succeed here and joy is yours in abundance.

Some years ago a big business man, sitting in a high-priced hotel, was approached by a friend, who said, "Sir, you should be very happy! You have built a great business and your name has become a national household word. You have succeeded honestly without any help or favors from your government. You should be happy, Sir, with your fame and fortune." The man's eyes dropped, his head bowed, he looked suddenly old and haggard. He said, "Yes, all you say is so. But what does it all amount to if the only boy you have is a fool?" There was no reply to make.

One can pile up his wealth if he lives frugally, works industriously and invests wisely, but what will it amount to if in the transaction one loses his boy? One can win fame, make his name great and become a political, civic or social leader, but what joy will that bring if, as you climb the ladder, your boy descends into degradation and shame? One of the most vital points of life is the relationship you sustain to that boy who calls you "Dad." If you fail there, life has closed every door of happiness to your soul. Give that boy your best and he will add to any joy that might be yours.

THE FATHER WHO CAME TO JESUS. After talking to the disciples, who were powerless to bestow a blessing, the father saw Jesus coming down the mountain and running to meet him, he fell down before him, and sobbing out his sorrowful soul, he said, "Lord, have mercy upon my son; for he . . . suffereth grievously; for oft-times he falleth into the fire, and oft-times into the water."

Three things we know about this boy. He was an only son, and how dearly the father must have loved him! Another thing, he had never been a good child. But, thank God, this unfortunate boy was blessed with a praying father. What a blessing is that! Do you ever pray for your boy? Did you ever go to Jesus in behalf of your son? Did you ever say, "Lord, have mercy on my son?"

We are told that this boy had a deaf and dumb spirit. It is very probable that his physical ears and tongue were all right, but he wouldn't talk and didn't hear. Your boy has this spirit if when you tell him to come back, he goes on as if you hadn't spoken. There are boys who will talk about everything—automobiles, airplanes, football, and so forth—but when you begin to talk about God, they close up like a clam shell. A dumb spirit strikes them. A deaf spirit comes and makes a boy self-willed, headstrong, stiff-necked, and disobedient. There are many other blighting spirits which possess boys. Let us name some.

The SPIRIT OF IDLENESS gets into boys. The boy who is reared not to work is headed for trouble. God's program for humanity is that a man shall eat his bread by the sweat of his brow. A man who attempts to eat his bread in any other way except by legitimate business and honest toil, breaks with God in his program for humanity. "Six days shalt thou work" is just as binding as the command to rest on the seventh. Paul says, "If any will not work, neither let him eat." The idle brain today, as it always has been, is the devil's workshop. In it he can make and perfect any scheme of hell that he desires. The greatest blessing a father can give his son is not to leave him some vast fortune nor some famous name but to teach him to work and to love it. Put into his soul a love for honest labor and he will not go far wrong in life. Keep out the spirit of idleness—it will wreck and ruin.

There comes also the SPIRIT OF PROFANITY. Boys sometimes think it sounds mannish, big, and smart to curse and swear and profane the holy name of God. Oaths and vulgarity flow out of their mouths like sewage out of a sewer pipe. This is the most worthless, silliest, and most uncalled-for sin that man can practice. The man who drinks gets a kick out of it; the man who steals gets what he steals, but the man who curses gets absolutely nothing from it. The devil baits his hook for every kind of sinner but the profane swearer. He is the sucker who swallows a naked hook. If the fathers would clean up some of their blasphemous, dirty, vulgar mouths and set a better example, we wouldn't have so much profanity among the boys. One reason there is so much profanity among boys is because they have such shining examples in their daddies. Like father, like son. Set your boy an example in clean speech and it will be worth a ton of exhortation.

Again, there comes the SPIRIT OF DRINKING. It seems

that most boys must see how it tastes and how it feels to be drunk. He begins by taking a sip socially—just to be one of the boys—he drifts into dram drinking and he finally becomes a drunken sot. No man ever intended to become a drunkard when he sipped socially. More deaths result from drinking among men of middle age than from any other one cause. In all my experience, I have never known a dram drinker to be worth much to the kingdom of God. I have known many fine, affable, generous-hearted men to be wrecked completely by this, the greatest curse of humanity. Whose institution do you believe in—the liquor seller or the preacher—the liquor store or the church? Which will you patronize? Who is doing your community the most good? Which do *you* now patronize and support?

Then, too, the SPIRIT OF GAMBLING develops in the boy. He sees it in the home where mother plays for prizes and hears it from his father in his friendly poker games. No wonder that gambling has become a national craze which threatens to engulf us! If I had a deck of cards, I would say, "Oh! you creature of idleness, around you the richly clad and beautifully robed women have spent many an evening of empty pleasure and foolish entertainment; over you many a blear-eyed, drunken gambler has staked the last dollar of a vast fortune that never returned.

YOUR HEARTS have been the means of breaking and bruising the hearts of mothers and wives who have waited late and watched anxiously for those who never came back!

With your SPADES, you have dug down and thrown out the last dollar of many a man's fortune and living, leaving him upon society an object of charity!

With your CLUBS, you have pounded thousands of men over the head and driven them like slaves to suicide and death!

With your DIAMONDS, you have etched the pictures of disgrace and shame on multitudes who never found life long enough to erase them. Away with you, thou fiend of hell and symbol of idleness, gambling, empty pleasure, and disgrace!

Again, the SPIRIT OF LUST enters our boys. This spirit is developed and fed in the dance hall. The dance craze is reaping a harvest now of immorality; if we could only know how extensive that harvest of immorality is, I am persuaded it would make us heart-sick. The long look should be had here as nowhere else. Nothing is more terrible than to have a disease germ that doctors tell us can never be wholly eradicated. The final harvest of this social sin is heart-rending. A young man brought his beautiful blue-eyed baby girl into an eye specialist's office and after careful examination by the doctor of the beautiful flaxen-haired girl's eyes, he turned to the devoted young father and said, "Sir! in two weeks your baby will be in total darkness." The father was stunned. He finally sobbed out, "Doctor, I ought to tell you that in my youth I wandered from the path of chastity and sowed my wild oats. I am wondering if this sore affliction of my child is a result of my sin." The doctor replied, "You need not have told me that. I knew it. Your baby will go through life in total darkness because of your sin, Sir!" The writer saw a baby girl in a hospital with one eyeball burst because of the teeming millions of germs that had infected her eyes, and it was all the physician could do to save the other one. Surely, if we knew the terrible results, we would fight this spirit of lust and keep these powers of the body sacred.

Look again, ruin is the final result of all these evil spirits. The deaf and dumb spirit of the boy, we are told, oft cast him in the water and in the fire. Satan is after your boy's life. He tried to kill Jesus before he got out of the cradle, and killed many two years old and under in Bethlehem. He tried to slay Moses when he was born, but God saved him through a mother's faith. He is after any boy or girl who has the background and opportunity of becoming a power for God. There is a big field to study right here. Satan's efforts to defeat the plans of God before his chosen servants are saved are, beyond question, most manifest.

FAITHLESS AND PERVERSE

This father and his generation failed in FAITH. Jesus said, "O Faithless and perverse generation." A perverse man is one who knows the right thing to do, but won't do it; the right road to take, but won't travel it. Any one of you fathers will admit readily that the thing you ought to do is to serve the Lord, give your heart to Christ, set an example in your home for God, but you won't do it. *You* are perverse. A faithless man is one who lacks the faith to pray, to read God's Word, and to witness for Christ in his family. The writer talked with a banker sixty years of age. He said that some day he intended to trust the Lord and confess him before men. "But when will you do it?" he was asked. Already he had passed middle life. When? Faith will lead you to do it. If you know the way, walk ye therein. If you believe, profess that belief and God will richly bless you.

"Bring him hither to me," said Jesus. Don't send him like so many try to do, but bring him. You can't send your boy to God, but you can lead him. A young man, facing the electric chair, was asked by the chaplain, "Mr. King, before the harness of death is placed on you, what last parting message have you for the mothers and fathers of this generation?" His reply was, "Tell them, Mr. Crain, not to try to send their children to Sunday school and church but to take them. My father tried to send me, but I didn't always get there. If he had taken me, perhaps I would not have landed here in the death-house." "Bring him," Jesus said. When Jacob got in trouble, he said, "Let us arise, and go up to Bethel (God's House)." No house in all the world is better than God's House to go to when distress of soul is on us.

The lack of our Faith—not the lack of God's Power, As the father brought his boy, he recited the whole pitiful story and said, "If thou canst do any thing, have compassion on us." Jesus said, "It is not a matter of my power but of your faith, for all things are possible to him that believeth." The leper came to Jesus and said, "If thou wilt, thou canst make me clean." This father doubted Christ's power to save. The leper doubted his willingness. But Jesus is both willing and able to save any man out of hell. He is able to save unto the uttermost all them that call upon him. No man goes to hell for any other reason than his own foolishness. "Where sin abounded, grace did much more abound." Jesus, who came filled with grace and truth, stands between any lost man and hell.

Notice the great compassion of Jesus. As this father tried to bring his boy to him, the boy was thrown into a spasm, wallowed in the dirt and foamed at the mouth. He must have been a dirty, loathsome piece of humanity. From the crown of his head to the sole of his feet, there was dirt and filth. Jesus, the immaculate, the pure and sinless, reached down and took hold of this loathsome piece of humanity and lifted him up. Surely he must have looked a blotch of filth and dirt. But Jesus will stoop down now and save the most loathsome and unclean soul that cries to him for salvation.

Christ has power yet to save. He can and will save and bless any one who may call upon him. If you are not the kind of father you ought to be, he can make you the kind you ought to be. Somebody has said that any kind of an old stick will do for a daddy but it takes a good woman to be a mother. This is absolutely false. The greatest man on earth in the sight of your laddie is the man he calls daddy. My boy used to come and put his little arms around my neck and say, "My good old daddy, my good old daddy." My prayer was, "Lord, help me to live so I may lead my boy aright." One evening as a father and his little son retired and were talking, as often they did, the boy said, "Daddy, do you know who the bestest woman in the world is?" He said, "No! I do not. Who is she?" The boy replied: "It is Mama." After a while he said, "Do you know who the bestest man in the world is?" He replied, "No, I do not," and was afraid to ask. But after a pause, he asked, "Who is he?" The reply came back, "It is you." You—father—can lead that boy of yours to the gates of glory or he will follow you to the portals of hell. Which will it be? Noah had the kind of religion that broke out in his family. He got all his family in the ark. Lot had the kind that made his children smile when he spoke to them about fleeing from the city of destruction. They laughed at him and said, "The old man is getting good." Give your wife a new husband and your children a new daddy. Christ will help you do that!

Life is largely a matter of sowing and reaping. The law of sowing and reaping obtains in the moral and spiritual realm as certainly as it does in the material. We reap what we sow. Some years ago the writer was in a series of meetings in a country church. One day the pastor and he walked out after the noonday meal and came upon an old house that looked as if it were ready to sit down. In it was a family with a blind boy. The house looked as if a lot of living had been done in it. So he asked the pastor, saying, "Whose old home?" The pastor replied, "This is the old B—family home." The writer knew that family— all of them physically strong men and women but most ungodly and wicked. The father was seventy years old and a notorious gambler. One son was a very profane man. Another son a double murderer. A daughter had married a bootlegger and she was hand in glove with him. As the writer stood before the old house and as he thought of that wicked family, he said, "Here is where the devil hatched out a brood and sent them out to curse and degrade the world."

A few days after that, the writer ate a meal with a family across the community. This, too, was an old family homestead. "Whose old home was this?" he asked. "This," they said, "is the old Edwards family homestead." The writer knew that family. The father was an old Baptist preacher and schoolteacher. One son was a college president, another a physician,

another a druggist. There were deacons, schoolteach-
ers, W.M.U. presidents and Sunday school officials—
all men and women of the highest type. "Here," the
writer thought, "is where God hatched out a brood and
sent them out to bless and serve."

How can you explain the great difference? One man
sowed to liquor drinking, Sunday desecration, neglect
of education and religious worship. He sowed to gambling and profanity and reaped a harvest that would
break any ordinary man's heart. The other man sowed
to education, to Sunday observance, to Sunday school
attendance, to the worship of God, to all things that
build Christian character and manhood, and he reaped
a harvest that would bring joy and gladness to any
man's soul.

One of the most terrible thoughts that ever entered
the writer's mind is that a father should open his eyes
in hell and find there his boys who had followed him.
One of the most glorious thoughts the writer ever contemplated is for one to pass into the eternal city and
find his boys there. "Oh! that would be great glory
for me." Surely this principle of sowing and reaping
explains why women predominate in the church and
men predominate in the penitentiary. Let us give ourselves, fathers, diligently to the sowing of the right
seed, and the harvest-time will bring gladness to our
hearts and joy to our souls.

FRIENDS IN BEHALF OF A NEIGHBOR

TEXT: They come, bringing unto him a man sick of the palsy, borne of four.—Mark 2: 3.

What a glorious thing it is to have good neighbors! One of the rich blessings of life is the fellowship of good neighbors. How poor any community is that lacks the fellowship of neighbors! Better than to *have* good neighbors is *to be* a good neighbor—a real friend to a neighbor. No man has ever yet been able to live to himself, and certainly no one can live to himself now. The supreme purpose of all lodges and brotherhoods, according to their charters and their vows, is not to take the place of the church, but their purpose is to make good neighbors out of their members. Any one who makes his lodge his religion is in the wrong place. The founders of the lodges never intended that they should take the place of the church, but that they should supplement the church and help to make good neighbors. One's "cable tow" as a lodge member might be a mile or a mile and a half, but as a Christian it is the distance between him and the man in need. That man might be on the other side of the globe. And his need might be spiritual—the sorest of all needs.

One of our greatest opportunities to witness for Christ is with our neighbors. If our neighbors are not better, nobler, and more devoted to Christ by having

(105)

lived by us, we are not the consistent Christians that we should be. Some years ago, an old Baptist preacher moved into town from his country home. He lived by an aged unbeliever who had also moved to town. After three years, one morning over the back fence, the old preacher said to his neighbor, "My brother, I have lived by you these three years. Are you a better man because of that fact?" His neighbor stopped hoeing his garden and after deep thought, he said, "I don't know whether I am or not." But in after years, the writer had the privilege of burying that same aged man in beautiful baptism with Christ. He said that the one who was used of God to make him think of his soul was a godly woman. One morning she asked him about his soul and urged him to settle it with God. But it is the writer's conviction that the background of that interest was the years of influence from the old Baptist preacher. Surely, if you are unable to reach your neighbors for Christ, your life is not what it should be.

How tremendously impelling is the example and influence of a faithful, loyal, consistent Christian! The story is told that in Alabama, a rich landlord, who had vast acres, had on his farm a peg-leg, ignorant tenant. The landlord was not a Christian and never went to the church. But the peg-leg, ignorant tenant was one of the most consistent, faithful and loyal Christians in all that country. Every Sunday morning, rain or shine, cold or hot, this peg-leg, ignorant tenant crossed the rich landlord's yard on his way to the church. He always had a Sunday school quarterly in his pocket, although he was unable to read a word in it.

For twenty years this went on. The rich landlord

could hear his tenant's peg-leg, thump, thump, thump, through his front yard. So one Sunday morning, the rich landlord went to church and at the close of the service, during the invitation, presented himself for church membership on profession of faith. His friends were utterly amazed and asked what influence, what person, what spoken word had caused him to come? His reply was that it was nothing they did; nothing the preacher said, or did, but it was the compelling power of example set by his peg-leg, ignorant tenant. He decided that if religion could help a man like that, it ought to be worth while to a man like himself.

One of the greatest opportunities we have to witness for Christ is on some cold or hot, disagreeable Sunday morning. If we fail to go to the house of the Lord and worship in his Name on such a day, we miss one of our greatest opportunities to witness for our Lord and to influence others for God.

There's a gospel according to you and men are reading it every day. Often it is the only gospel they do read. What kind of a gospel are you offering your neighbor? Somebody said, "One man living a brotherly life is worth a thousand lectures on brotherhood." One Christian, consistent in his daily walk, is worth ten professional soul-winners.

There is positively no need of having bad neighbors. If you have such, kill them—that's what you feel like doing!—and make good neighbors of them. Some one tells the story of a farmer who came into a new community to look over a farm. He was thinking of buying it. As he looked it over, one, living on an adjoining farm, came over and said, "Sir! if you buy this farm, you can't live on it. Your adjoining neighbor will make life miserable for you." The prospector replied if he bought the farm, he would move on it and if his neighbor bothered him, he would kill him. This man, wishing to make peace (?) between neighbors, straightway went and told the bad neighbor what the prospective buyer said. His reply, with a snarl, was, "We'll see who gets killed first."

The farm was bought. The man moved on it and things soon began to come to pass. The new neighbor's cows got out in the bad neighbor's oats. The bad neighbor took his gun and killed one and sent word for the new neighbor to come and get it. He brought the cow home, dressed it and sent the bad neighbor a big round steak. Soon, the new neighbor's hogs got out and damaged the bad neighbor's corn. He sicked his dogs on them and crippled one so badly that it had to be killed. The new neighbor dressed it and sent a big mess of sausage over to his bad neighbor. When the new neighbor's children passed the bad neighbor's house, he would curse and abuse them and chunk rocks at them. When the bad neighbor's children passed the new neighbor's house, he came out, patted them on the head, spoke kindly to them, and gave them red stick candy to eat.

This went on for some time. But one can't resist always such a friendly spirit. One day, in the spring, as the bad neighbor hauled his fertilizer home from town, he was passing by his new neighbor's house. Just as he got in front of his house, a wheel crushed under the heavy load. There he was—most embarrassed!—unable to get away from a man who had been most gracious to him. That is a most embarrassing situation to be caught in. Soon he saw his new neighbor approach. He said, "Friend, I have a wheel here that I will never use and you must have it." He got his old wagon wheel and helped him put it on. Just before the bad neighbor crawled up in his wagon, he said, "When you came here, I heard that you said if I bothered you, you would kill me. I want to say that you have pretty nigh done it with kindness!" And so it was!

God says, "If thine enemy hunger, feed him; if he thirsts, give him drink; for in so doing thou shalt heap coals of fire on his head. Be not overcome of evil, but overcome evil with good." When one returns evil for evil, all he does is to add to evil. Two wrongs never made a right. You can't fight fire with fire. You simply increase it. But you can fight fire with water. Never try to fight evil with evil, but fight it with good and the victory one day will be yours.

In our scripture, four men had a neighbor who was a paralytic. What is more pathetic than a paralytic! Surely this man must have been about middle age. His condition must have resulted from sin. Instead of being a blessing to his family, he was a burden. Instead of being wings, he was a weight. How deeply he must have repented of his sin as he lay helpless from day to day on his bed! This sorely afflicted neighbor was greatly blessed with four friends. They got together and said, "We must take our neighbor to Christ. He will greatly bless and make him a blessing." If the four *"right"* men should get together, they could take to Christ any lost man to be found anywhere.

Let us look at these four men. They were this neighbor's warmest and truest friends. Who are your real friends? Your answer might be those with whom you chum and are most congenial. But those might be your worst enemies. If they seduce your soul and tempt you to do wrong, they are your enemies. Your friend is one who keeps you on tiptoe; who brings out the best within you; who frowns on all that is wrong in your life and approves that which is right.

Surely, if you knew that one had threatened your physical life, you would guard yourself against that person. But some will chum with and seek the company of those who, they know, will assault and seduce their immortal souls. Some years ago, a man who had been given to heavy drink, sought a place in a city government. He was finally appointed to the position. One man, offended by his appointment, offered fifty dollars to any one who would make this newly appointed man drunk. Soon the man was seen driving out of town in an automobile with the worst enemy he had, the one who had offered the fifty dollars award for getting him drunk. One who saw him, said in his heart, "Good-bye, old man, you're gone." In a short while, the word went out that the poor fellow had been found in a drunken condition. No one has a greater enemy than the man who will put a bottle to his lips and tempt him to drink; who will seek to degrade one's soul and whose influence over him is blighting and damning. Seek your real friends and cling to them. They will bless and lift and strengthen. These four men were real friends to this paralytic neighbor.

Again, these four friends would be today members of some church. Salvation is not dependent on church membership. There are some who say they are saved but not members of any church. Such, in my opinion, are few and far between. I have never seen any one lead another to Christ who was not himself a member of some church. Soul-winners are found in warm fellowship with some of God's people. There are freaks of nature and there might be freaks of grace. I've seen a two-headed calf. There might be saved people without church fellowship. Who knows? A saved person out of a church certainly must be a spiritual freak. To say the least he is abnormal. If you would bring another to Christ, get in fellowship with some other Christians and work in close harmony with them.

Again, these four friends would be members of some church in their local community. One of the keenest problems faced today by the churches of volunteer relationship is the unaffiliated member. We today are truly a people on wheels. Never before has one's residence been so uncertain. Many things in civilization contribute to this state of affairs. Because of this fact, people should form the habit of moving their church membership wherever they go. So many fail even to reach their own children when they neglect their local church affiliation. Some years ago, the writer, soon after entering upon the pastorate of a great church, was approached by a man most anxious about his elder son. He wanted the writer to help get his son to Sunday school and church service. The writer asked the father where his membership was. He replied that it was one hundred miles away. "How long have you lived here?" he was asked. "Ten years," he replied. He and his wife were both non-affiliated members. They were most splendid people. He was told that nothing would be done to reach his four children until he and his wife did their duty. "Why!" he said, "Do you think it would make any difference?" "Certainly, it makes a great deal of difference," he was told.

Soon they brought their membership and placed it in the church. The four children were baptized. He became a deacon and the pastor's warm friend. Some years afterward, he carried his family seventy-five miles to hear the writer preach and had him out to dinner. That's further than the writer would drive to hear himself preach! When he did his duty to the church, God blessed him with his children.

Oh! you may think it does not matter, but God organized the church to keep the spiritual pulse of his people beating strong for his Kingdom. No great soul-winner will be satisfied to live long in a community without becoming a vital part of the religious life of the community. Surely these four friends would be found today close up and forming a vital part of the religious life of the community in which they lived.

Look what Christ will do for a neighbor brought to him. He will speak, first, a word of good cheer. "Seeing their faith"—not their wealth, not their culture, not their position in society—but their faith, he said, "Son, be of good cheer." It is needless to say to one, "Be of good cheer" unless you can say also, "Thy sins be forgiven thee." Where does one find cheerful looks? Certainly not behind jail bars. When business seeks a sweet, radiant face for mother's day, where does it go to find it? Certainly not from those who have dissipated and spent their lives in the service of sin. Cheerful looks are found on the faces of those whose hearts are right with God. Sin causes the lines of the face to drop. The Bible is as up-to-date as if it were written yesterday. God said to Cain, "Why is thy countenance fallen?" Scientists perform an operation today which is called "lifting the face." One woman

I knew paid a thousand dollars to have her face lifted. It was a most ungodly looking face—a smile that *couldn't* come off. With such a woman for a wife one couldn't tell whether she was angry or pleased. It was lifted mechanically. It can be lifted naturally. The tap-root of ninety per cent of the misery of this world is sin. Cheerful looks are found only on the faces of those whose hearts are right with God. Grace in the heart means lines of happiness on the face. "They looked unto him, and were radiant."

Second, Christ will speak the word of forgiveness. "Thy sins be forgiven thee," he said. These carping critics that day were right once when they said, "Only God can forgive sin." When Jesus spoke the word of forgiveness, he spoke as God. That prerogative belongs to God and to God alone. Will you consider? Wrongdoing related to society is vice. Society can pass over or frown on vice as it wills. (There is nothing more isolating than a frown on vice from society.) Wrongdoing related to the state is crime. The state can punish or pardon as it sees fit. But wrongdoing related to God is sin, and only God can forgive sin. Every time any priest says to a confessor, "I absolve thee," he speaks an untruth. None can forgive *sin* but God only. A spiritual adviser can urge one to seek forgiveness and can tell him how to seek it, but God must forgive, if sin is ever forgiven.

Thus if one's sin is a crime, he may suffer and pay the state for his crime all the length of his life. But if the criminal does not deal with God for his sin, his sin will weight his soul in hell. David cried, "Against thee and thee only have I sinned, O God!" Only God can blot out sin. In his sore temptation, Joseph cried,

"How can I do this great wickedness and *sin* against God?"

Our chief relationship in this world is with God. You can't live ten minutes without God. Close your mouth and nose. That's God's air you are breathing. God made us, he feeds us, he gives us breath and life and blesses us with strength and health—all come from God. He is the good and perfect giver. The depth of ingratitude is to breathe God's air and curse the name of God with the very air you breathe; to eat God's rations and to use the strength you get from them to serve Satan; to walk on God's earth but never to walk in God's way. Certainly this is the depth of ingratitude. But however ungrateful a soul has been, God will forgive when we come confessing.

Let me ask, what is forgiveness? Jesus said, "That ye may know that the Son of man hath authority on earth to forgive sin." Forgiveness is not sweeping aside penalties which come in this life as results of sin. David confessed his sin, and God forgave, but David reaped results right on. The only punishment for sin the Christian will receive is in this world and this explains why many times it seems that the godly suffer more than the ungodly. If we sin, we must suffer, because sin sooner or later always brings suffering.

Forgiveness is nothing more nor less than the continuous and uninterrupted flow of love toward the one who has committed the wrong. It is God saying to every repentant soul who cries to him for mercy, "My child, there is nothing between us but love." Some while ago, a boy wronged his father. The father was hurt deeply but said little about it. Soon the manly boy felt that he had wronged his father and being sorry, he came and said, "Dad, I'm sorry." The father turned with deep emotion in his voice and said, "My boy! I'm glad you said that. There was a chasm between us, but it is all right now." Surely, God, who is love, will speak the word of forgiveness to any soul as it falls prostrate before him and cries, "O God, I am sorry." God, in his great mercy, comes and picks such a one up in his everlasting arms and says, "My child, I love you." "Your sins are blotted out as a thick cloud. They are removed from you as far as the east is from the west. Your sins, they are no more." Christ said that he has power on *earth*—not in heaven or hell, but on *earth*,—that's where we live,—to forgive sin. If that poor paralytic that the four friends brought to him, got up and carried away his bed, his sins were forgiven. The story says that the people were amazed as he obeyed.

Obedience should follow forgiveness. God always gives the power to do what he bids us do. Like the old Negro who said if God commanded him to jump through a brick wall, it was his business to jump and God's business to remove the wall. Jesus spoke to the paralytic and commanded him to arise and take up his bed and walk. As he began to obey, strength surged in his emaciated body. The condition of salvation is faith, and the test of faith is obedience. What joy, what power, what happy feeling comes as we step out on the Lord's side after the word of forgiveness is spoken to our souls! Some years ago in a very difficult series of meetings, the writer one Sunday morning approached publicly the pastor's son about his soul. This the writer seldom does in his ministry. But that morning there was no move from the audience and, being so anxious, he spoke to the pastor's fourteen-year-old son as he stood very near the front during the invitation. The boy refused to move from his tracks. After the service, the writer returned to the pastor's home where he was a guest. As he entered, the wife came with her face bathed in tears and said, "You'll have to excuse us. We are all broken up." The writer at first thought perhaps her feelings had been hurt because he had gone publicly to her boy during the morning service. But she continued by saying, "Tom is sorry that he did not go this morning. He has promised that he will seek and confess the Lord tonight." That night Tom came. It was a beautiful confession of faith. His face was radiant, and yet as he poured out his heart tears of repentance flowed down his cheeks.

When Tom opened his eyes the next morning after a restful night's sleep, his mother tells that the first thing he said was, "Mother, I feel the best this morning I have ever felt in my life. It looks as if I am in a new world. Everything is so beautiful!" Yes! he should have felt the best that he ever felt because he had done the greatest thing any man ever did—committed his soul's welfare to God. The world looked new because there was a new world in his own heart. Jesus is even now ready to speak that word of forgiveness as he did to the paralytic brought to him borne of four. If you will call upon him, he hath said, "Whosoever shall call upon the name of the Lord shall be saved."

THE GREATEST STORY EVER TOLD

TEXT: When I see the blood, I will pass over you.—Exodus 12: 13.

One of the most fascinating stories in all the Book is the narration of the glorious deliverance of Israel from the galling bondage of Egypt. You know the story of how Joseph was sold into slavery by his brothers. From slavery, for no cause of his own, he was cast into prison. Then, by the grace of God, he was lifted out of prison and became the prime minister of the greatest empire of that day. In the course of events, trailing the dream of Pharaoh, the severe famine came on. Joseph's father and family were forced to send into Egypt for corn. After two trips, the whole family moved into Egypt.

What a warm welcome was accorded Jacob and his family by Pharaoh! Surely, no greater welcome was ever extended to any popular hero. Pharaoh gave them the privilege of the best of Egypt. The rich, fertile, well-watered land of Goshen was to be their home. Here they were to live, rear their children, and build their homes. The devil has always been most profuse and cordial in his welcome to those who come into his territory. The most cordial handshake used to be at the door of the saloon—one of the entrances to hell. When the prodigal son arrived in the far country with his pocket full of money, he must have been warmly welcomed. The devil always serves his best wine first. The further you go in his service, the worse it becomes. The dregs come last. God serves his best wine last at the banquet of life. The further you go with God, the sweeter life becomes. Jacob was warmly welcomed by Pharaoh into Egypt.

Here in the goodly land of Goshen, the sons of Jacob reared their families and multiplied rapidly. They made their living easily and unmolested. After a while Joseph, the youngest son, prime minister and savior of Egypt, died. Like men everywhere, Egypt forgot Joseph and his merciful ministry. Then Egypt began sorely to afflict Israel. Heavy burdens were laid upon them and after a while they became abject slaves. How ungrateful is the unregenerate heart! How soon they forgot! Tex Rickard, the great prize-fight promoter of New York, said some years ago that he had paid out to prize-fighters two million five hundred thousand dollars and not one single man had ever turned and said, "I thank you." If the unregenerate soul forgets God, shall we be greatly surprised if he forgets the kindness and ministry of God's servants?

When this bondage of Egypt began to gall and grind and bind and blister, Israel was driven to her knees. Sorrows and hardships are always merciful if they push us to our knees. "When they had prayed," God began to work out his plans of redemption and deliverance. And what marvelous methods he used! The first item in his program was to bring into this world a beautiful baby. If God or men are to do much, they must begin at the cradle. This baby was kept three months and nobody knew he was around. Some time ago a baby lived across the street from the writer and nobody knew that anybody else was around. When Moses was three months old, his godly mother, by faith, made a little ark of bullrushes. She lined it with pitch and the softest of downy material. She also put in it faith and love and trust and hope. Then she placed tenderly her beautiful babe in it, and carrying it she placed it on the bosom of the Nile River.

There were crocodiles in that river that could have swallowed that baby at one mouthful. But when the mother put her babe on the bosom of the Nile, she laid him in the everlasting arms of God. No child is safe anywhere that has not been committed to God. Every child who has been given to God is safe anywhere. Like Samuel, given by his mother to the Lord, Moses by his mother was committed to God.

This mother knew exactly where to place the babe. The daughter of Pharaoh came to bathe in the Nile—a religious ceremony. The little twelve-year-old sister of Baby Moses was properly stationed and told to await developments. If that had been some twelve-year-old girl today, the mother wouldn't have known where she was in ten minutes' time.

After a while a beautiful Egyptian princess came with her maidens. As she started to perform her religious rites, she saw a tiny ark among the reeds. The maidens drew it out and lifted the lid. There in that little ark was the most appealing thing in the world to a true woman's heart—a beautiful Hebrew baby with big tears rolling down its velvety cheeks. This princess said, "I will make this my baby." Miriam came to the princess and said, "Would you like to have a nurse for your baby?" And she replied, "That I would." Then Miriam said, "I know where the best nurse for that baby in all the world is." Soon the mother was on the scene. She had never been very far away. Then Pharaoh's daughter said to her, "Take this child away, and nurse it for me, and I will give thee thy wages." Did one ever hear any story more romantic than that? The devil tried to kill Moses. The state had issued a decree saying that all Hebrew babies must die. But God saved him and gave him back to his mother to nurse and had the state to pay her for this ministry to her own baby. It would have been gracious to have just the privilege of nursing him, but God is most gracious and he arranged for the state to send her its official check every month. How wonderful is God's goodness!

The next item in God's program was to *educate* and *train* his deliverer. If we are to be much, we must know much. God can use an ignorant person but he can do so much more with one well-trained. After some years with his mother, Moses was started to school in Egypt where he learned all the arts and sciences of his day. If Moses was to be greatly used of God, he must be thoroughly trained. Two of the greatest mountain peaks in history, excepting, of course, Jesus, are Moses, who was learned in all the wisdom of Egypt, and Paul, the Apostle and missionary, who was one of the most thoroughly trained men of his day. God can use in his service any man who consecrates his life to him. But be not deceived, he can use to far greater advantage a well-trained soul. Yes! Moses must have the best that the world could give in order to fulfil the mission God was to send him on. For forty years he was in training.

MOSES, A POSTGRADUATE. After finishing the courses in the university of Egypt, God wanted him to take a postgraduate course in the mountains of Midian. Here for forty years more, he studied God, studied himself, his people, his promises, and the country through which he was to deliver his people. Moses must know the topography of that land. He must be familiar with every trail, with the location of every spring and water course, and with the direction of every mountain range. Here for forty years he moved slowly up and down this country with his sheep. It was a lonely, dreary life, but God was training him.

The next item in the program was to get Moses "STARTED AT HIS TASK." The time had come when God was ready, the people were ready, and Moses was ready. As he led his sheep one day in the back of the desert, God spoke to him in a burning bush and commanded him to go back and realize the great desire of his heart—"Deliver my people, Israel." At first he begged to be excused, but finally he consented. Thus, Moses, at the court of Pharaoh, with Aaron as his spokesman, begins the royal battle. God must melt a hard, stubborn and flinty heart, or break an iron will. How tenacious and stiff-necked was Pharaoh! But this arrogant ruler said to Moses finally, "Bless me also."

The next item is the PLAGUES. Ten terrible plagues were brought on Egypt. God begins with water turned to blood. Everywhere there had been water there was blood,—blood in basins to bathe, blood in cups to drink, blood in tubs to wash with,—blood everywhere there had been water,—ponds of blood, rills of blood, rivers of blood.

Then there came the frogs,—frogs jumping, frogs croaking, frogs everywhere. Sit down at the table and a big old frog would jump in your plate. Go in the living-room and a big old frog would be found in the easy chair. Go to bed and stretch out your feet and a big old frog would be touching your toes. God said they were in the kneading troughs, and when the curse was removed and the frogs died, they were piled up in piles and stank. Much of the land of Goshen was marshy and like a delta. And this plague of the frogs there was not at all unreasonable.

Then there came in quick succession the lice, the flies, the murrain, the boils, the locusts, the hail, the darkness. Each time Pharaoh's heart became harder. One more plague awaits and Egypt will beg Israel to go. Even Pharaoh, who stood like a wall of granite against all of God's terrible judgments, will beg Moses, saying, "Bless me also." God will not save any man against his will, but he can bring any sin-hardened soul to his knees and compel him to plead for mercy. Pharaoh cried, "Bless me also."

The next item is the final TEST. Before they go, God must put his people to the test to see who had faith and who had not. This was a very simple test. Each family, or two, where families were small, must provide a lamb, perfect as a lamb can be, without spot or blemish, on the tenth day of the month and keep it until the fourteenth day. While slaying this lamb on the fourteenth day they were to draw its blood in a vessel and dipping a bunch of hyssop in the blood, they were to strike it once over the door and once on each side—three simple strokes would do! Any family could do that. In that house with blood on the door, they were to roast the lamb whole and eat it with their loins girded, shoes on their feet, and staff in their hand.

It is easy and quite natural to imagine that God called Gabriel and said, "Tell the death angel to get his hosts ready to fly over Egypt on the night of the fourteenth day. Tell him, Gabriel, to visit every home in the whole land, from that of Pharaoh in his palace to the captive in the dungeon. Gabriel! tell the death angel to watch for the blood. He will find it on the side posts and over the door. Gabriel, tell him to pass over every home where there is blood and enter every home where there is no blood and smite the first-born male of the home."

I can imagine that Gabriel tells the death angel to make ready for his flight. The day arrives and heaven is intensely interested and watches closely the preparation being made by Israel for the visit of the death angel and their deliverance.

BEHOLD THE LAMB! Heaven watches as the people slay the chosen lamb without spot or blemish—perfect as a lamb can be. Here's the symbol of the Son of God. Years ago, as they went on their way up Mount Moriah for sacrifice, Isaac, the only son, bearing the wood, asked Abraham, his father, saying, "Where is the lamb?" and with trembling lips he replied, "God will provide the lamb, my son." Here God provided the lamb in symbol. Years afterwards, Isaiah caught a prophetic view of the lamb and described him minutely in the fifty-third chapter of his divine prophecy. Now let us stand with John on the banks of the Jordan, and after he baptized one from Nazareth, he bears true testimony, saying, "Behold the Lamb of God, which taketh away the sin of the world." Here is the true lamb God has promised and provided.

Look again! Here also in Egypt is the cross as plain

as plain can be. Place a cross, with blood on its head-piece and blood on the two armpieces, against a door frame and see the perfect fitness of it! Christ on the cross surely had blood on the head-piece, for he had been crowned with thorns. There was blood on the arm-pieces, for the nails had pierced his hands. Behold the Lamb!—the innocent, the spotless, the chosen Lamb of God!—the suffering, slain Lamb of God.

FAITH REVEALED. The heavenly host looked on as the people took a bunch of hyssop, a common herb of Egypt, and dipped it in the slain Lamb's blood, struck it once over the door and once on each side. I can imagine that the angels cried to the Son of God, saying, "What's that they are doing?" "That," said the matchless Son of God, smiling, "is faith. Faith applies the blood. That reveals their trust. They believe that God's Word is true and that his plan of salvation will save them from the judgment of God. That! That is faith!"

Thus they watch the death angel as he directs his hosts, flying with lightning speed over Egypt here, there, and yonder. They pass over the houses of Israel where there is blood. Behind the blood, each family is happy and free and eager and ready to go. Oh! what joy there was and what a feast they had that night! They sang, they shouted, they praised God. It was like a revival meeting. They were free. The very moment they applied the blood they became free. Never again would they feel the sting of the task-master's lash on their back. Never again would they bend their backs to the burdens of Egypt. Tomorrow's sun would rise on them on their way to the promised land. It was almost too good to be true. It was more like a dream than a reality.

But wait! look! there's a house and a home without the shed blood. They did not believe that God would do what he said. How terrible is the sin of unbelief, doubt, and indifference. The death angel enters this home of unbelief and finds the firstborn lying sleeping, dreaming of his day's play. He snaps the brittle cord of life and goes on his awful mission. The child struggles, gasps for breath, and writhes in death agony. He mourns a pitiful mourn and the death-rattle is heard in his throat. He cried, "I am dying. I am dying." He wakes his parents. They rush to him and work frantically over him, but he is soon gone. Oh! what sorrow and grief!

The death angel goes on and leaves in his wake, where there is no blood, no sadness and bitterness and blasted hopes and death. Look! in Pharaoh's ivory palace the queen mother holds the lifeless form of her firstborn in her arms, her heart sobbing a sigh of sor-row. Yonder in the back alley, in a hut, sits a mother in rags, holding her firstborn with the same sharp arrow of grief plunged deep in her heart. Thus the heavenly hosts turn to the Son of God and say, "O matchless Son of God, you see what difference the blood makes, —how it saves from tragedy and sorrow and brings joy and peace and happiness!" The Son of God smiles and says, "Yes! in the fulness of time, I will go and shed my blood that there may be remission of sin."

GOD LOOKS FOR THE BLOOD. The blood is what God looked for then, and is what he looks for today. Some say that they do not believe in the innocent suffering for the guilty. They call Christianity a slaughterhouse religion. But whenever you find a man whose opinions differ from God's Word, there is something wrong, not with his head but with his heart. The inconsistencies are found not in the Bible but in the lives of men who will not accept the truth of God's Word.

God did not say when I see your honesty or conscientiousness, but when I see the blood. Conscience is no sort of a safe guide. It may be, and is as often wrong as right. It must be quickened by God's spirit and guided by his truth. Before the flood, God left the whole race to their conscience, and all went down except Noah and his family. Before the flood, not one single moral law was given, not one moral precept. Conscience is not sufficient. Many a man is in trouble today because of his wrong opinion. One can believe in the wrong thing as easily as in the right. It makes a world of difference what one believes. No greater lie was ever perpetrated by Satan than that it does not matter what you believe. Brother! believe in the blood, and it will save.

The blood stands for God's hatred of sin. One thing no man ever argued about and that is the reality of sin. There is argument about the Bible being the Word of God; about Jesus being the Son of God; and about the reality of hell and heaven, but no one ever argues that there is no sin. The blood, too, reveals the black, damning consequences of sin. Seen through the blood, sin stands out in all its hideousness and vileness. Sin made the Cross of Christ a necessity. Only sin and the love of God can give any reasonable explanation of the Cross. If man had not sinned and God had not loved, Christ would not have died. But man did sin, he became depraved, and God loved and "God commendeth his love toward us, in that, while we were yet sinners, Christ died for us." The blood reveals the hideousness of sin and commends to us the love and grace of God.

GOD LOOKS FOR THE SHED BLOOD. It was the shed blood that saved Israel in Egypt. It is the shed blood of Jesus that saves from sin now. That's the only basis on which God proposes to forgive sin. Does he not say, "Without the shedding of blood, there is no remission of sin?" If Christ could have saved by his matchless moral precepts, by his wonder working miracles, or by the supreme example of a perfect life, it would not have been necessary that he die. God could have taken him as he did Enoch, or translated him as he did Elijah or buried him and his grave as he did Moses. But Christ must give his life a ransom for many. He must shed his blood. He must taste death for all men. The blood must be shed.

This completely, absolutely, without shadow of doubt, does away with the idea and principle of salvation by any other means. One cannot be saved by reformation, for all are corrupt; nor by morality, for no one is good; nor by ceremony,—form without power will not help; nor by good works. It is "by grace are ye saved through faith; and that not of yourselves; it is the gift of God: not of works, lest any man should boast." Self-made men are usually very self-centered men and most difficult to approach. If one could save himself, he would be the greatest object of curiosity in the world, and most boastful. Only faith in the shed blood saves.

GOD IS LOOKING FOR THE APPLIED BLOOD. The shed blood must be applied. It must be applied individually. In Egypt the unit in God's sight was the family, but now "Each one of you must give account." Every one must apply the blood for himself. There is no proxy in matters religious. There can be no brothers-in-law nor sisters-in-law nor godfather nor godmother religiously. Every one is individually responsible to God. All through the Book, this one great truth is taught over and over again. The soul that sinneth must die and the soul that applies the shed blood shall be saved.

This clashes and completely annihilates the doctrine of Universalism. The false doctrine of Universalism sets forth the principle that since Christ died for all men, all men will be saved. Surely this is a subtle snare of Satan! His blood was shed for all men and all men may be saved, but God says, "He that believeth and is baptized shall be saved; but he that believeth not shall be damned." The gospel is the power of God unto salvation to EVERYONE THAT BELIEVETH." Christ is able to save unto the uttermost "THEM THAT COME UNTO GOD." The gift of God must be accepted, the blood must be applied.

The blood is applied now as it was applied then— by faith. Those who believed that the death angel was coming on the night of the fourteenth day and trusted in God's plan of salvation, applied the blood. Those who did not believe did not apply the blood. God's curse was upon Egypt as it is upon the world. Faith in the shed blood removes the curse and impending judgment of God and brings grace and blessings that abide forever.

The blood must be applied before the visit of the death angel. Some say they mean to apply it some day. Why do men put off and delay what God says is so important? God says this year. You say next year.

God says this month; you say next month; God says this week; you say next week; God says today if you hear my voice, harden not your heart. And you say tomorrow. Pharaoh said tomorrow. Thousands have said tomorrow, but they never reached the tomorrow. Why not now? "Why do you wait, dear brother?"

When the fourteenth day of your little life is at hand and death stands knocking at your door, I know you will want the shed blood applied. When the shadows begin to fall and the darkness of death closes in on us and we feel death's clammy breath blown in our faces, our cry will be "Lord, abide with me." When the two disciples on their way to Emmaus reached the end of their journey, they constrained Jesus, saying, "Abide with us: for it is toward evening, and the day is far spent." Yes! when this little life's day draws to a close, we shall want Jesus.

Suffer one illustration. In the death-house of a southern state waited one who had murdered his business partner for insurance. He was sentenced to die. He did all he could to have that sentence commuted to life imprisonment. But it was useless. The day of execution was set. And when he faced death and realized he must die soon, he spent every waking moment studying and reading God's Word. Would that he had been thus busy earlier! As he waited for the day of execution, some sympathetic club women, thinking to do the condemned man a kindness, carried him some magazines and said, "Sir, we felt that time would hang heavy on your hands and we have brought you some reading matter." The man looked up from the Book and said, "I thank you, lady, for your intended kindness, but there is only one Book for a dying man, and I am reading that Book every waking hour." Yes! the blood of his fellow man was on his hands, but he wanted the shed blood of Christ on his heart.

Faith in the shed blood saves from sin. The only institution redeemed in this world is the church. Paul said to the Ephesian elders, "Feed the church of God, which he hath purchased with his own blood." Christ did not save a chamber of commerce, nor a lodge, nor a school, nor even a home, but he bought the church with his own precious blood. Church membership does not save, nor does church ceremony, but if we are saved we will want to be in the church with saved people. I am a member of a church and shall remain a member in good standing as long as there is a New Testament church. If my church should withdraw fellowship from me this Sunday, I would come and knock at their door next Sunday. If they still refused me fellowship, I would knock the next Sunday. No man nor party can deprive me of the joy of being one of God's people in the one organization that Christ purchased with his shed blood.

Faith in the blood breaks the power of sin. The story has been told of one who came to this country to exhibit a great python snake. These snakes, which grow sometimes to be sixteen feet long and kill by wrapping round their prey, are most manageable and docile when not angry. But their grip when angry is almost certain death. One man in a zoo was caught in a python's coils and it took eight men to loosen the snake's grip and free the man. The man, who came to this country with his snake, appeared before a great audience and was going to show what the great snake could do. When the showman came out on the stage with his python, it was very evident that the snake was angry. After telling something of the history and training of his snake, he stepped back, snapped his fingers and the snake rapidly coiled around him. He petted it and plead and begged and soon the snake loosened. He threw it to one side. One man in the audience arose and begged him to cease his exhibition. He replied that he knew his snake and would go on. The snake was lying at one side coiled with its forked tongue sticking out and its eyes flashing fire. The man stepped up and snapped his fingers and before one hardly realized it, the snake was around him, gripping like death. He plead and begged and stroked its body and patted its head. It gripped tighter and tighter, until his face became flushed. But soon the snake loosed its terrible coil and the master threw him to one side.

The people rose en masse and demanded that he cease, saying that they realized the snake was angry and it would mean death to go on. The man replied that he knew his business and knew exactly what he was doing. If they would attend to their business, he would attend to his. The snake was coiled with its tail flapping the floor and eyes snapping fire and its forked tongue sticking out. The man stepped up and snapped his fingers. The snake almost jumped at him. Coiling around him rapidly, it began to grip. Tighter and tighter it gripped. He plead and begged and patted it on the head but it gripped tighter. He gently stroked its body but the snake gripped tighter. The man's face flushed red like crimson as the snake gripped tighter. The blood vessels on his face and neck stuck out like great cords as the snake gripped tighter. The audience saw him reel, they heard a crack and the death rattle and he fell headlong on the floor as the snake gripped tighter and broke every bone in his body.

Oh! You can go into sin once and come out. It may grip your soul twice and yet throw it off. It may grip three times and again throw it off. But one day sin, like the python, will grip your soul unto death and will break every noble principle and leave you ruined and wrecked and ready for humanity's junk heap. There is power in the blood. It will break sin's hold upon your soul. It will make you a free man in Christ Jesus.

The greatest story ever told by human lips is that story that never grows old. The more we hear it, the dearer it becomes. It is the story of God's love and Christ's sacrifice on the old rugged cross. Open your heart and feel its power, by saying with Charlotte Elliott:

> Just as I am, without one plea,
> But that Thy blood was shed for me,
> And that Thou bidd'st me come to Thee,
> O Lamb of God, I come! I come!

THE WORST THING IN—

Text: All unrighteousness is sin.—1 John 5 : 17.

Those who read the First Letter of John must be impressed and struck, along with many other fine things, with his short definitions. He gives two definitions of God that have never been surpassed by all the philosophers and theologians since or before John's day. Listen to these.

"God Is Light, and in him is no darkness at all." God is the source of all light. He said, "Let there be light, and there was light." God's Word is a lamp to our feet and a light to our path. God's Son is the light of the world and is the true light that lighteth the way of every man who comes into the world. This old world would be a dark and dreary place in which to live if it were not for the light divine that is shed on our way. We would grope in the darkness as the heathen who know not God, but "God is light, and in him is no darkness at all."

Another short definition—"God Is Love." This is the first great fact the child learns about God. This is taught in the Cradle Roll Department and in the Nursery. This was a new revelation of God to man. Men have thought of him as a God of wrath and of anger and of judgments. They had seen him in the storm and wind and affliction, but had failed to see him in the

(133)

sunshine and showers and in the daily blessings of life.

GOD IS LOVE, and all his dealings with men are compassionate. "All things work together for good to them that love God." GOD IS LOVE, and he sent his only begotten son to die on a cruel cross that we, poor sinners, might be saved. GOD IS LOVE, and he sends the Holy Spirit to woo and win our hearts to Jesus. GOD IS LOVE, and he sends his rain and sunshine on the just and on the unjust. We ought to shout every time we think of God's great love. He so loved that he gave the greatest of all gifts to a ruined and lost world.

Notice again, "All unrighteousness is sin." The writer speaks here of "a sin unto death," and says that for those who have committed such a sin we should not pray. This sin unto death is, I think, the sin against the Holy Spirit. It cannot be forgiven in this world nor in the world to come. This sin is committed when one continues to say, "No! and no! and no!" to the wooing of the Holy Spirit. The Holy Spirit is a Person and, being a Person, he knows when one has made up his mind not to accept Christ. Most people who come to sell anything to the writer know when he has made up his mind not to buy. Once in a while a book agent seems to have a little difficulty in deciding when one has made up his mind not to buy. But the Holy Spirit is an intelligent Person and surely knows when one says, "No!" and means "No!"

This "sin unto death" is a sin against the Holy Spirit and can never be forgiven, for when one sins against God the Father, he still has God, the Son. When one sins against God the Son, there is still left to woo his heart and intercede for him God the Spirit. But when one sins against the Holy Spirit, he is left alone and there is no hope, because one must be drawn if he finds God.

"There is a sin unto death: . . . and there is a sin not unto death." There is a sin that can be and will be forgiven if we come seeking "the Lord while he may be found, call ye upon him while he is near." There is sin that God will blot out as a thick cloud and remove from us as far as the east is from the west. "All unrighteousness is sin."

I. What Is the Worst Thing Here?

1. It is not Poverty. I can well imagine you have some poverty here, though I have not seen many signs of it. To be poor is indeed unfortunate. I would hate to become an object of charity in my old age. One serious objection my father had to my entering the ministry was that I would be a poor dependent in my old age. Many old preachers are. Dire poverty is sometimes brought on by unfortunate circumstances and sickness; but ninety per cent of the dire poverty of this world is a result of sin. Ninety per cent of the inmates in the almshouses are there because of sin. This statement was made in a pulpit some years ago and one of the leading citizens resented it, because in early life unfortunate circumstances caused him to be an inmate of an almshouse. But after reflection he said to the pastor, "My Brother, you are right. The women inmates of the almshouse when I was there were the devil's old hags." It seems if a woman could make money, she might do so by selling herself over the counters of wickedness. But that's the type which comes to old age penniless and poverty stricken. Sin's tendency is to produce poverty.

There are others who are not objects of charity but

who are called "poor." God has greatly used men and women who have come up through poor circumstances. Nearly all of his great servants have come to maturity through hard circumstances. God says, "To this man will I look, even to him that is poor and of a contrite spirit and that trembleth at my word." Call the roll of the great spiritual leaders—Martin Luther, Savonarola, John Huss—and see where they came from. How many millionaires' sons do you know now preaching the gospel? One, "Borden of Yale," was so unusual that a book must be written of his college days and activities.

Unfortunate as it is to be poor, there is more real joy to be had with Christ and a crust of bread and water than to be without Christ and have a table laden with the dainties of the world. Yea! more joy is had with Christ and the plainest of gingham dresses than to wear the finest of silks and satins and be without Christ. The things of this world, however fine and abundant, do not bring joy and satisfaction. The rich fool found out that one cannot feed his soul with "much goods." Dives learned that life does not consist in the abundance of things of this earth. Poverty, as bad as it is, is not the worst thing.

2. IGNORANCE is not the worst thing. It is an unspeakable tragedy for one to come to maturity in body with an undeveloped and untrained mind. There is no reason now for any one in this country not to have the rudiments of an education. The state is spending millions of dollars; six million women and one million men are giving themselves to the task of training the minds of our boys and girls. This money, this time, and energy are all well spent.

Mind is a marvelous blessing, and not to train it is a tragedy. But some of the greatest souls, most consecrated characters, have been those who had little of this world's knowledge. You may possess all the knowledge the world can give and use it for evil purposes. Some think that the most important matter for their children is school, but of far greater importance to a child is the knowledge of God. When you educate a crook, you simply multiply his capacity for crookedness. When you educate a fool, all you have is an educated fool. There is nothing finer in this world than to see a well-trained, highly cultured man or woman consecrated wholly to the Lord and to his Cause. Culture and consecration are two of the greatest combinations ever to keep company in one soul. There is nothing much worse, more blighting and deadening than to see one with a highly trained mind given wholly to the service of Satan. Far better to know little of this world's knowledge and serve the Lord than to know all and use this knowledge in the service of sin. No! Ignorance is not the worst thing.

3. AFFLICTION is not the worst thing. How dreadful it is to be afflicted! How would you like to be blind, or deaf, or dumb, or crippled, or hair-lipped? How often we have occasion to appreciate the blessings of a strong body! One very deaf, a shoe-cobbler, one day asked if I would write him out a prayer. I asked Why? The reply came saying that in all his life, he had never heard another pray. He attended church occasionally but so deaf was he that he could not hear those who led in prayer.

The afflictions and diseases of the body so touched the heart of Jesus that he healed all those who were brought to him. But Jesus said that affliction is not the worst misfortune. If thine eye, or hand, said Jesus, offend thee or cause thee to stumble, pluck it out or cut it off. It is far better to enter life with one eye and one hand than to have both and be cast into hell. If we should pass on the street one afflicted, diseased, and with body warped, we would pity such a one and perhaps toss him a coin, but we pass those who are on their way to destruction and even become associated with them in business or pleasure and never one time are we concerned about their lost condition.

The greatest misfortune is not to be deprived of these physical eyes, but to lose spiritual insight and fail to see "the Lord high and lifted up." This tongue might be dumb and silent, but if there is a song in the heart and a soul full of gratitude to God, this is acceptable to him. Some of the greatest notes of praise we have ever heard, came from those who seemed to us to have little to be thankful for. There is more joy with Christ and an afflicted body than to be without Christ and have the halest, healthiest body one may possess. No! affliction, as bad as it is, is not the worst thing.

4. TROUBLE is not the worst thing. How many hearts are there broken, bleeding, bruised, and crushed! Some one has said if he were God and knew all the sorrow of the race, it would break his heart. One good woman, as she sobbed out her sorrow, said, "There is something in here broken and I feel that I will never be the same again." Her sorrow took her appetite, robbed her of her sleep, and finally sent her to a hospital. There are many who are burdened with sorrow; all you need do to start the tears flowing is simply to mention their trouble. How our hearts ache for those burdened with deep trou-

ble! When the clouds gather and the shadows crowd in on our souls, how hard it is!

Every one feels that his or her trouble is the worst. One couple who had built a beautiful home and had planned for a family of four, was sorely troubled when just before they moved in, the boy was taken by death. They had bought their rugs and draperies. Everything was ready. Then came the heart-breaking sorrow of losing their fine boy. The wife said she didn't believe the Lord intended for them to have the beautiful home because he killed all the joy there was in it. The husband was so deeply grieved that he stayed away from his business. His family and friends became uneasy about him. The pastor went to talk frankly, and as he approached the subject of their great sorrow the father burst into tears and said, "Oh! Sir! our trouble is the worst that can be. No one else has ever suffered like we." The pastor replied, "Your trouble is not the worst. Yours is a dead trouble. What about those who have living troubles?" I would rather look at my boy's face any day through the lids of a casket than through the bars of a jail. "Oh, that our father had died a year ago so he would never have known the disgrace of this crime!" was sobbed out by a devoted daughter on the death of her honored father, whose son had killed two men.

The hope of those who have trouble is to "cast thy burden upon the Lord, and he shall sustain thee." Trouble is like a baby, the more you nurse it the bigger it gets. Trouble will pass as the years come and go. Time and the grace of God will heal many broken hearts. It will leave a scar. But all trouble brings a child of

God closer to his Heavenly Father. No! trouble is not the worst thing.

II. The Worst Thing Is Sin

1. Yes, black, slimy sin; bright, dainty sin; deadening, damning sin; secret, hidden sin; open, public sin. Sin is the terrible curse of humanity. What a tragic statement is made in the third chapter of the "Book of Beginnings"! We read how sin entered the world and death through sin. God had created the universe. He had placed the sun in his tabernacle for light by day and started the silvery moon on its course for light by night. Then he dotted the sky with millions of twinkling stars. Then he made the world—its flowers, its fields, its birds, its beasts. He created the seas, the lakes and rivers, its hills, plains, and mountains. He fixed the seasons in their order and sent the rain and sunshine. The earth brought forth its fruit. The succulent grass grew, the flowers bloomed, the trees bore their luscious fruit and the grain became golden with harvest. "And God saw everything that he had made, and, behold, it was very good." He was highly pleased. Then out of the dust of the earth he made man, and breathed into his nostrils and "man became a living soul"—the climax of creation. He gave man a beautiful helpmeet and placed them in a fertile, productive, and beautiful garden to keep. Then man, his chief creation, sinned. And through him, heinous and cruel sin entered the world. It must have broken God's heart to see this— his master-stroke of creation—sin.

2. Look at the Genealogy of sin. "Lust, when it has conceived, beareth sin: and the sin, when it is full-grown, bringeth forth death." The lust of the eyes, and the lust of the flesh are just one step removed from

death. Sin is the child of lust and the father of death. David, the beloved king yonder in the palace, walked out on his roof one day and looked at a woman bathing. He looked once, he looked twice, he looked three times. And sin soon stalked into the palace, showed its ugly form and revealed its terrible power. And sin,—David's sin, full-grown—brought forth death. It looked as if David's life was too short to finish reaping the full harvest of this dreadful sowing. Death, one death after another, came, and removed one member after another of the royal family. There was the death of Uriah, his faithful soldier; of the beloved child of sin; of Abijah, at the hands of Absalom; of Absalom, at the hands of Joab. What terrible tragedy followed and grew out of the lust of David's eyes!

3. Consider the DESTRUCTIVE POWER of sin. It will cause anybody, anywhere, anytime, under any circumstances, to fail. Somebody has said in words similar to ours that it will ruin business. The witnesses are plentiful enough. Call them to the stand and ask them why their business went on the rocks. They will tell you that once the future was rosy with promise. Customers and clients were numerous. They were busy and hopeful and expectant. But something happened. Trade declined. Clients and customers grew less. Business became dull. The expense was greater than the income, and finally they were declared bankrupt and the doors locked. The details might vary in each case of failure, but the primary, basal cause was the same. Sin came, the public lost confidence and becoming disgusted, turned away.

Sin ruins nations. God says that righteousness exalteth a nation, but sin is a reproach to any people.

The greatest enemy of any nation is not some outside foe, but rottenness within. Rome was never conquered until she became rotten at heart. Babylon, Egypt, Greece, Rome, and Persia all were once flourishing nations. Each ship of state was sailing with its sails full of the wind. But sin came and killed the Albatross; their sails dropped down and they rotted in their own wickedness. If our great nation, whose flag has never been furled in defeat, ever goes on the rocks, sin will put it there. Some years ago a picture came out with Uncle Sam being served by the beautiful young woman "Luxury." In the shadows stood armored Rome, who whispered in Uncle Sam's ear, "Be careful, Samuel. Luxury was once my mistress." I tremble when I hear of political corruption, official graft and greed among high officials of state. Surely we are drifting too near the precipice over which other nations plunged to destruction.

Sin will destroy every vestige of a home. This fundamental institution in our civilization is safe so long as sin does not interfere with it. But when sin comes in, peace and happiness go out. Confidence and fellowship are broken, love and mutual trust wither and die and the home ceases to be. But what produces this condition?

Poverty has never destroyed a home. The great per cent of divorces are granted not to the poor but to the rich. The house may be an humble cottage or cabin, the furniture may be little and cheap, and the floor may be bare of rugs and the windows without draperies, but it is home, sweet home, if the voice of the loved one is music to the beloved's ears. And "Be it ever so humble, there's no place like home," where there is love and confidence and peace and fellowship. But break this, destroy this, ruin this and the vestibule of heaven is turned into a vestibule of hell. Sin will do that.

Sorrow and misfortune never wrecked a home. Where a man and his wife love each other, the greater the sorrow, the closer are they drawn together; the greater the burden, the lower they bend their backs, and closer the co-operation. A tiny babe, three weeks old, was left in an old couple's home. A daughter had died and left this tiny baby girl. It was a great sorrow. For years before this sorrow, the old couple seemed to have been drifting apart. But this tiny baby girl reached out and got hold of their heart-strings and in a short while they were more considerate of each other and were more affectionate. A new joy came into their home and a new light into their eyes.

Keep sin out of your home. Only one thing will push a man and his wife apart. Sin will come and scatter a home like a cyclone. It will drive the members of a family in every direction and will transform any home from a heaven into a hell.

III. But What Is Sin?

1. Let God answer—"All unrighteousness is sin." God says "all," and that means "all,"—every form and fashion of unrighteousness. If you would know what sin is, ask this question, "Is it right?" Judged by the Word of God, "Is it right?" How will it look yonder before the white light of the judgment throne of God? Ask this question of your inmost soul, "Is it right?" If it is not right, it is sin.

There are certain well-known common vices that all men label "unrighteousness." We readily admit that the acts of lying, stealing, drinking, gambling, and murder are unrighteous. We seldom make a mistake in labeling sins of commission. But there are sins of omission which are just as damning and hurtful as sins of commission. God says, "To him that knoweth to do good, and doeth it not, to him it is sin." Sin is unrighteousness; sin is always "unrighteousness," and all unrighteousness is sin. If it is not right, it is sin. Let us ask.

2. Is it right to live in a community for any length of time, receive the blessings of a church, enjoy the atmosphere that such churches create, rear your family and conduct your business in a Christian community, and withhold from that church the greatest gift you can make to it, which is the gift of the influence of your example? Is it right to stand aside and apart from the church and fail to give it your fullest co-operation? No wonder so many who sin in failing to move their church membership, grow cold and indifferent and many times never warm up to the cause of God again. Some excuse themselves by saying they are not SETTLED. But when is one settled? Not until God settles his soul in eternity and his body in the ground. Does any one wish to become settled? Then let him make it known and we will pray that God might settle him.

Others excuse themselves by saying they do not know whether they will STAY or not. How long have you lived in the community in which you live? Some years ago we asked a couple about their church membership and why they had not placed it in the church of the city. The reply came that they did not know whether they were going to STAY or not. "How long," asked the writer, "have you been here?" "Oh," they said, "six years." "Well," we replied, "You are not going to STAY, you have already STAYED." Why will people of God move into a community, receive all the blessed benefits of a church and refuse for years to give to that church their greatest gift—the influence of their example and the warm co-operation of their heart's interests? Is it right? If it is not right, then it is sin; and sin always produces death and sorrow of heart.

3. Let me ask again, Is it right to stand out and apart from the uplifted, bleeding form of the Son of God whose arms are opened wide ready to receive any and all who will come believing? See his side—it is all marred with a thrust of the spear. See his body—it has been smitten and bruised for *you*. See his feet—they have been pierced with nails for *you*. See his hands—they have great deep gashes made in them for *you*. Surely the poet could sing:

> See, from His head, His hands, His feet,
> Sorrow and love flow mingled down;
> Did e'er such love and sorrow meet,
> Or thorns compose so rich a crown?

Oh! you may think you are a pretty decent, moral person and not guilty of many things that others do, but the sin of unbelief, the sin of rejecting the Son of God, will sink your soul in hell. You can crucify the Son of God on a cross of indifference as surely as they did on the cross of wood. There is no sin in all the catalogue common to man that is more cruel than that of unbelief. A little woman came into the pastor's study, wringing her hands in a frenzy, saying that she never slept a wink the night before and she just had to come and sob out her sorrow to some one. After quietly talking to her, she poured out her soul saying that her husband had come home that night and said he didn't believe in her. He doubted her. It broke her heart. It cut like a knife, it struck like lightning and bruised like a scourge. How brutal is the sin of unbelief! How cruel is the sin of cold indifference!

4. Yes! all unrighteousness is sin. But sin may be forgiven. It can be blotted out as a thick cloud. God says, "Come now and let us reason together . . . : Though your sins be as scarlet, they shall be white as snow; though they be red like crimson, they shall be as wool." Jesus is here now and is ready to forgive and speak the word that will lift your load. If you whisper in his all-hearing ear the prayer of the publican, "God be merciful to me a sinner," or if you will cry to him as the dying thief, "Lord, remember me," he will say as he did to the paralytic, "Son, be of good cheer; thy sins be forgiven thee," or to the timid little woman who touched the hem of his garment, "Thy faith hath made thee whole." Will you do it? Will you do it right now? The worst thing anywhere is sin; but God will forgive. "The blood of Jesus Christ his Son cleanseth us from all sin."

THE MAN DOWN AND OUT

TEXT: He would fain have filled his belly with the husks that the swine did eat: and no man gave unto him.—Luke 15: 16.

Come and let us find our way out into the field among swine and interview a man. Let us realize that some time ago, we do not know how long, this man we are to interview left his father's house with a high head, a proud walk, and a pocketful of money. He took the trail that leads to the far country, and soon he was in it. The situation with him has greatly changed. Behold him now in a most miserable condition,—destitute as any man ever came to be. He is feeding hogs, with the filth and odor of the pen upon his clothes. Now, with him, there is no regular boarding house with nice, clean, wholesome food, because his meager wages will not permit that necessity. There is no comfortable room nor warm, soft bed to rest his tired and weary body, for that, even, is a luxury beyond his reach.

What awful regrets must fill his soul! What terrible remorse must gnaw at his heart as he remembers sometime ago his "riotous living" when he threw money away like a drunken sailor! But look at him now! His hat is of the finest brand, but it is so greasy you could make soap of it. His shoes are of the highest grade, but they need half-soling, shining, and new strings. His shirt is woven of soft silk, but it is split and torn and sorely needs a trip to the laundry. His trousers are from the best clothiers and made of most expensive fabric, but they sorely need a trip to the cleaners and somebody to patch the ragged holes and sew on the missing buttons. Ah! like the man who was passing from Jerusalem to Jericho, he had fallen among thieves, had been stripped, robbed, and left destitute. So terrible is this man's present condition that he fain would have filled himself with the husk the swine did eat, and no man gave unto him.

The husks here spoken of were pods of the carab tree, which thrives along the Mediterranean coast and are used as feed for cattle and sometimes eaten by the poorest of people. The picture presented here is that of one subsisting on whatever food he might find. Today such a one would be at the mercy of the public, begging from house to house. In our larger cities, he would be found feeding from the refuse of hotels and restaurants. His food now consists of scraps and left-overs. What a terrible condition sin brings one to! This horrible picture of a man feeding swine and desiring that which he feeds them is, to the refined and sensitive soul, disgusting, repulsive, and nauseating. But Jesus, the most sensitive and purest soul that ever men looked upon, is the one who paints this horrible word-picture for us. I would like to have seen the expression of utter disgust on his face when he said, "He would fain have filled his belly with the husks that the swine did eat: and no man gave unto him."

In this marvelous story of matchless beauty and simplicity, Jesus is saying to us in the plainest possible sort of language that the tendency of sin is toward the hog-pen; that all sin, of whatever sort or nature, leads in that direction. Every man and woman who goes into sin does not come to this state of poverty and degradation, but that is the tendency of all sin. If you are living in sin, playing with it, embracing it and walking in its ways, you are on your way to wretchedness. You may never reach it, but this man and thousands of others did. If you live long enough and travel fast enough, you will reach the hogpen on schedule time. That's the end on this earth of that miserable way.

But the sorest results of sin are not physical. This man not only had his feet in the pigsty, but, worst still, his heart's affections were there. He not alone had the odor of the pen on his clothes and person, but, far worse, his thoughts were unclean and unholy. His garments were not only torn and ragged, but there were confusion and conflicts and unrest in his soul. His physical needs were simple and could easily be supplied, but his inner and deeper needs were far greater and more difficult to meet. Supply one's deeper, inner needs and he himself will ordinarily supply the simple, temporal necessities. Yes! sin brings destitution.

Ella Wheeler Wilcox has said:

> I gave a beggar from my little store
> Of well-earned gold. He spent the shining ore
> And came again and yet again, still cold
> And hungry as before.
> So I gave a thought, and through that thought of mine
> He found himself, the man, supreme, divine!
> Fed, clothed, and crowned with blessings manifold
> And now he begs no more.

By permission, W. B. Conkey Company, Chicago.

Another has said:

Coulds't thou in vision see
  Thyself, the man God meant,
Thou nevermore could be
  The man thou art, content.

Three Kinds of Poverty

There is MENTAL poverty. There are great areas of this world where ignorance, vice, and superstition reign supreme. People know nothing of themselves, of the forces of nature about them, nor of the God who made them. Disease in such sections reaps its harvest of death without protest. Insanitary conditions are never remedied, and life becomes one long period of misery and wretchedness. This is the dire result of mental poverty. Such people need science to wave its magic wand over them, their homes, and their country to make life worth the living. Knowledge is a sore need among those of mental poverty.

Again, there is MORAL poverty. When men and women do not regard the sacred bonds of matrimony; when the social disease lays hold and from it one can never fully recover; when people drink and gamble and waste all their earnings; when they so live that no respectable employment is open to them; when they murder, kill, and destroy, leaving tragedy and sorrow in their wake; when they lie, cheat, steal, and defraud and their word is no more than a passing breeze; and when they slander, malign, and vilify, breaking and bruising the hearts of their friends and neighbors—that is moral poverty. How poor such people are! In this world's goods they might be millionaires, but they are paupers in the graces of happy living.

Again, there is SPIRITUAL poverty. When men and

women have no desire for God and his Cause; when they rob God, withholding from him the tithe; when they never hunger nor thirst for righteousness; when they never erect an altar nor offer a prayer, nor lift their hearts to God in praise for his many mercies; when they consider the church a burden; the worship of God a bore; the songs of Zion nonsense; the Book of God a puzzle; the preaching of his truth, foolishness; the proclamation of the gospel of Jesus, wind-jamming; that is spiritual poverty. The rich fool had "much goods," but he was poor and bankrupt toward God. Many supposed to be decent and respectable people are terribly poverty stricken spiritually!

What brings all this poverty upon us? We answer with one word—Sin. More is said about the poverty of this prodigal son than any other phase of his being. A famine was on. His last cent was gone. He had spent all. He was hungry. No man gave to him. He was in dire need. Jesus is trying to tell us about sin and show how poor we become when "we live riotously." It is impossible to paint with words the whole terrible picture. It beggars description.

How unhappy this poor fellow must have been! Happiness is determined not by conditions without but by conditions within. Bars do not a prison make. The great difference between happy and unhappy people is not on the outside but on the inside. A great deal of our hell will be of our own making. A young woman had been sent to an institution because of wrongdoing. One day she ran away from the institution and a preacher was asked by her mother to locate her. He found her, and after praying and pleading and reading, he said, "What about it?" She answered that she would do anything but go back to the institution. He said, "Marie, your trouble now is that you failed to do as your mother wished, isn't it?" She answered in the affirmative. The preacher plead some more and read more, then he pressed for a decision. She said, "I will do anything but go back to that institution—it is hell over there!" The preacher said, "Marie, you found your home hell, didn't you?" "Yes," she answered. "You will find hell everywhere you go until you change inside," said the preacher. How can we find heaven on earth when we have hell conditions in our souls? The prodigal son found his greatest poverty not without— sore as that was—but within. The source of his great misery was not primarily because he would have filled himself with the husks the swine did eat but because he had cast to the winds those things which make for happy living.

What This Man Needed

He needed more than reformation. A social reformer might have worked with him a thousand years, but such a one would never reach and remedy the primary cause of the trouble. Reformation has never lifted man yet out of his deepest trouble. The sow always returns to the wallow and the dog to his vomit. You may drive nails in a plank and pull them out, but one thing you can't pull out—the nail hole. Regret and remorse have never yet undone the wrongs of a soul. Reformation is simply a soul feeding on husks hoping that they will finally turn into meat and bread. The bread that cometh down from heaven can only be had at God's mercy-seat, not in a pigsty.

This man's greatest need was not food or clothes, but

manhood. Character can be sold for naught, but it cannot be bought back at any price. To be a man, dependable, trustworthy, generous-hearted, and open-minded, faithful in every relationship, is the greatest achievement of life. Playing the part of a real man is what makes one's name valuable at the banks, in the market place, and at the council table. The three C's of all good credit are: Character, Capacity, and Collateral. Let any one lend money on these and he will be certain to collect. And the best security of all is Character.

This man needed a good name. God says, "A good name is rather to be chosen than great riches." Some years ago, it has been said, a sales bulletin stated that the board of directors of the California Fruit-growers' Association admitted that the seven-lettered name "Sunkist" was worth ten million dollars to the fruitgrowers of Southern California. The Regal Shoe Company has admitted its brand is worth two million five hundred dollars to them. Cluett, Peabody and Company, estimate their "Arrow" trade-mark is worth fifty-four million dollars. What an asset is a good name! One of the great needs of this prodigal was a good name. Once he had it, but in riotous living he lost it. Sin will rob a man of the most prized assets of life and leave him with nothing but liabilities.

Notice again—"No man gave unto him." We do not need the Bible to tell us that when a fellow is down and out the world is through with him. Look about you and this fact may be verified a thousand times. It is easy to find friends who will help you spend your money, but when it is all gone, the friends become few and far between. But hunger, want, and poverty are a blessing if they but drive us to God. The quicker this man's bread is gone, the sooner he will become serious and think on his way; the sooner he will come to himself and return to his father's house. If this man's father had continued to send him money and to supply his physical needs, he would never have come to himself. Acting on this basic principle, we ought never to give the professional tramp and dead-beat money. When we do, we say by deed, "Old man, you go on your way bumming and I will help you pay your expenses." Many a dead-beat and bum ride their way through life on the sympathies of tender-hearted people who think they are kind in helping them. But in supplying their physical needs and wants we encourage them in their wickedness and waywardness. God's program of "sweat on the face before bread in the mouth" would rid the world of ninety per cent of its dead-beats.

But the poor we have with us always, and there are many unfortunate souls who must be cared for. The church is the greatest source of charity in the world. While the lodges get credit for much that is done, the real source and spring of benevolence is the love of God in the hearts of men and women.

This man finally came to himself and said, "I will arise and go to my father, and will say unto him, Father I have sinned against heaven, and before thee: . . . make me." But many thousands who travel the broad and downward way of sin, never come to themselves. They die in their sins. They go out like Judas, and "It was night."

There seems to be something horribly fitting when a man who has lived in sin and fed his soul on the husks of iniquity, dies under sinful conditions. Some years ago the writer was in a revival meeting, and one afternoon was being shown around the little town. He was driven out by the house which once was the home of the community's richest citizen. That family was composed of the father, mother, a son and daughter—all were very wicked and depraved. It is said that one local citizen, who was given to cursing, went one day to have the noon meal with this family. As they all ate together something went wrong. The father became angry and began to curse. The mother was crossed and began to curse. The son took up the quarrel and began to curse, and finally—God forbid—the daughter took sides in the family fuss and began to curse. This visitor afterwards said he thought he knew something about cursing himself, but in that terrible atmosphere of profanity and swearing and anger he became frightened. He never entered the beautiful home of the richest and most wicked man of the community again. As my friend and I drove on around, we came upon a log cabin on one of this rich man's farms. The host said, "There is where our richest man died." "You mean your richest man died in that dilapidated log house?" I said. "Yes," came the reply, "he was here looking over the farm and found the Negro tenant and his wife in a fight. He pulled his pistol to strike the man over the head and accidentally it went off. He shot himself. They carried him into the cabin. His blood was in such a terrible condition that blood poison set up and before he could be moved, he died." The writer said, under his breath, "There is something horribly fitting about a death like that." Thank God, many come out from the wretchedness of sin. But, sorry to say, many others die under most horrible circumstances. What a pity to die in a drunken stupor; to drop dead in a dance hall, or to come to the end of your way in a gambling den! God never planned any life to end like that!

In New York City, it is said that a hotel chambermaid found the dead body of a young man in his room one morning. By his side was a piece of folded paper which proved to be his last will and testament. It was legibly written and bore the marks of culture. But sin had wrought in his life. The note, proving to be his last will and testament, read, "I leave to society a bad example. I leave to my father and mother all the sorrow they can bear in their old age; I leave to my brothers and sisters the memories of a misspent life; I leave to my wife a broken heart, and to my children the name of a drunkard and suicide; I leave to God a rebellious soul which has insulted and defied his loving mercy."

There are two processes in this world. One is that of life, the other of death; one is integration, the other is disintegration; one is ascent, the other descent; one is the process of growth and improvement; the other is the process of deterioration. These two processes are taking place everywhere and in every realm. Sin, in its process of degradation, will rob a man of all that is human and leave him more of a beast than a being. The sin of cunningness makes a fox out of a man; the sin of brutality makes a snapping wolf out of a man, and the sin of greed and filth makes a hog out of a man.

Many have been found in the hogpen. Some years ago, the writer preached a series of sermons from the story of the prodigal son. He delivered this message one Sunday evening, and on the following Monday morning, he met the Chief of Police and asked him

what he did the day before. The Chief told of finding three men on Sunday evening about nine o'clock in
an office building. They had been there all afternoon,
gambling and drinking. The Chief tried to describe
the filth of the whole scene and as words failed him,
the writer said, "Chief, did it look like a hogpen?"
He replied that it looked more like a hogpen than
anything he had seen in a long time. The writer said,
"Yes! While I was yonder in my pulpit last night
trying to preach on the man in the hogpen, you found
three in it." Surely sin brings misery, wretchedness,
and degradation! No man can be at himself—his
higher and better self—and go in sin. Surely he must
be beside himself to continue long in sin. For sin
is the most unreasonable and insane course in life a
man ever took. It fills one with spiritual lunacy and
moral idiocy.

Thank God for those who come to themselves and turn
to God. Many leave the husks the swine did eat and
go back to the father's house where there is bread and
to spare. The story is told of a young man who left
his home to go into a city to make a name for himself
and build a life. Before he left home, his mother
placed her hands upon his head and said, "My son, remember as you go to the great city that every night at
nine o'clock I'll be praying for you." He left with this
benediction of his mother. After arriving in the city,
he soon fell in with a crowd whose feet traveled the
same road as the prodigal son. Some months afterwards, when this young man with his companions
passed hurriedly down the street, the clock in the tower
struck nine. He stopped. They went on. Immediately they missed him. They looked back and he was

standing stock still where he had suddenly stopped. They called to him, saying, "Come on, we are late now." He shook his head and replied, "I am sorry, but you will have to go, if you must go, without me." They said, "Why! what's the matter? What's come over you? Come, there's just one girl for each and you must go with us." They turned back and taking hold of him, they started to pull him on. Protesting vigorously, he said, "Wait, and I will explain. Just now the clock struck nine. When I left home, my mother put her hand on my head and prayed for me. Her parting benediction was that every night at nine, she would be praying for me. I can feel her hand now resting on my head. I must go back. I cannot go on." He turned and went back, never again to walk in the road that leads to wretchedness.

Oh! if you have wandered! If your feet have left the path of rectitude and righteousness; if you find yourself treading the way that leads to wretchedness and misery —the way that the further you pursue it the darker, more dismal, and harder it becomes,—stop, and think before it is too late! There is another way. It is the path of the righteous,—a way that becomes brighter and more beautiful the further you go. It is the way of the dawning light; the way that leads out on the upland; that ascends to the hill of the Lord—to his Holy place. Yes! He will lift us up out of the miry clay, put our feet on the rock, establish our going, and put a song in our mouth. He will walk by our side. Will you begin now to travel the new and better way?

REASONS FOR LIVING

TEXT: To this end am I come into the world, that I should bear witness unto the truth.—John 18 : 37.

Life, fraught with such vast opportunities, must have a chief end. There must be some reason for existence. The first question asked in the shorter catechism of the Presbyterian church is: "What is the chief end of man?" That question is answered, "To glorify God and enjoy him forever." I find that every creation and product of man's hand is made for some specific purpose. The electric light, automobile, radio, telephone, zipper, and cotton picker. Each was invented and designed for a specific purpose. Man has never been so foolish as to make anything for no particular purpose. Thus God must have purpose as he creates life. Surely life with all its potential power must have purpose.

Unless life is a humbug, there must be a reason for every individual life. Perhaps you have heard of that group of students who tried to play a joke on an old biology professor. They went out and found the wings of one bug, the legs of another, the head of another, and the tail of another, and put them all together. They carried this strange specimen to their beloved professor and said, "We found this strange bug and, being unable to classify it, we want you to help us." The bug was placed carefully by the old professor under the micro-

(159)

scope, and after a minute of deep study he turned back with the seriousness of death on his face and slowly said, "Young gentlemen, this is a humbug." But life is no humbug. It is not a farce. There is meaning and purpose for every life. It is said that some noted actor as he passed into the shadows cried, "Draw the curtains, the farce is over." To discover the chief end of life and to make life purposeful is a long step toward making life worth while.

God must have a definite purpose for every life. It is said of Queen Esther, "Thou art come to the kingdom for such a time as this." If Esther had failed in the high purpose that God planned for her, life would have become tragic for thousands of her fellowmen in Babylon. It is said of Paul, "He is a chosen vessel unto me, to bear my name before the Gentiles, and kings, and children of Israel." What a marvelous missionary this bitter, persecuting protagonist of Christianity became after he struck the high road that God would have him take! "GOD WILLS IT" is the master motive of all life. "God wills it," and Joan of Arc was transformed from the timid maid of Domremy and became the conquering spirit of the discouraged French army, driving the English soldiers from her beloved French soil. "God wills it," and Oliver Cromwell, the praying Puritan, was transformed into a thunderbolt striking down ancient wrong. "God wills it," and one crusade after another broke like a mighty tidal wave against the walls of the Moslem hordes. To be possessed with a conviction that "God wills it" and to be willing to be used in carrying out his will, will transform any life from the mediocre and humdrum to that of ecstasy, beauty, and glory.

Let Us Look First at What We Are not Here for

We are certainly not here to live for SELF. I find that I am a member of a family, a citizen of a city, a state, a nation, and a member of a church. See how our relationships widen and enlarge. Being a member of a family gives me domestic obligations. Being a citizen of a city gives me civic obligations. Being a member of a church gives me spiritual and moral obligations. If my family needs my money, time, thought, or energy I would be a poor sort of a husband and father if I did not give freely and liberally of what I have. If my state demands my life, it has a right to conscript me and to use me in defense of its rights. If my church needs me or what I have in time, money, thought, or energy, it has a full right to expect me to supply its needs so far as my little life can do so. There are far too many giants in the business and social world and too many pigmies in the religious realm. Paul felt deeply his obligation to all men when he said, "I am debtor." What a generous spirit was his when he declared that he was ready to discharge that debt so far as his life would permit! We are debtors to all men who need our ministry. We are indeed and in truth our brother's keeper.

We can make our lives living channels of blessing, or they will become poisonous and bitter, dead seas.

> Is *your* life a channel of blessing?
> Is the love of God flowing thro' you?
> Are you telling the lost of the Saviour?
> Are you ready His service to do?"

"Ye are not your own, for ye are bought with a price," and

Somebody else needs a blessing.

.　　.　　.　　.　　.　　.

We'll let our lights shine
To His glory divine,
Somebody else needs a blessing.

There is entirely too much suffering and sorrow, too much poverty and destitution for men and women to draw themselves in and become as close as a clam.

If Jesus had come to live for self, he would have turned the stones into bread; he would have lived in an ivory palace; and would have ridden with his flowing robes of purple in a golden chariot. But there were others, and those others in need obligated him. Their sore need so burdened him that at times great tears coursed down his cheeks as he contemplated their need.

Life is indeed too complex and too closely related for any man to live to himself. The head cannot say to the foot, nor the five-talent man to the one-talent man, I owe you nothing. The man who lives on upper main street in his brownstone front, wearing his diamonds, riding in his Packard automobile, cannot say to the man on lower main street who is jobless, hungry, ragged, and dirty, I owe you nothing. These two men, however far apart socially they may be in the extremes of society, are closely and vitally related in a thousand different ways. The welfare of one is the welfare of the other.

The story is told of a rich landlord who cared only for collecting his rent from his many poverty-stricken tenants. He had a beautiful daughter. She was planning an elaborate wedding. An order was given a merchant for a fur coat. The work on the coat was farmed out to poor seamstresses. When the day arrived for the wedding, this beautiful daughter was deathly sick of spinal meningitis. They wondered where the terrible disease came from. They began to trace the germ and discovered that as the beautiful fur coat was farmed out, a poor, widowed seamstress, who lived in one of the rich man's houses, had worked on it. As she sewed on the beautiful coat, her child was ill with high fever and chills. She threw the costly coat over the child to make it comfortable. That child had spinal meningitis. The germ was carried from the hut on the back alley all the way into the ivory palace of the rich landlord. How closely and vitally they were related!

Again, we are not here for the mad pursuit of PLEASURE. No pleasure is ever obtained by pursuing it. Pleasure is like a butterfly, we weary ourselves in the chase and never catch it. Some people remind me of a little poem found in my *Holmes' First Reader* when I was a boy, which read as follows:

> Six little rabbits
>   Went to run
> Up hill, down hill,
>   Oh! such fun!
>
> Jump, jump, jump,
>   See how they run,
> Up hill, down hill,
>   Oh! such fun!

It is run here and run there and jump, jump, jump until one becomes tired and weary of the dizzy, dazzling, mad pursuit after the pleasures of this world. Our nerves crack and leave us a wreck when we should be in the prime of life. So many get on the social merry-go-round and ride and ride and ride until they become groggy and dizzy, losing all interest in everything else except the social merry-go-round. They ride it six days a week and crowd it on the seventh. They get off right where they got on. They haven't moved one single inch, nor traveled one single foot of distance. No wonder the pleasures of the world become as insipid and tasteless as branch water in the summertime or spigot water in the city.

There is a thrill in a merry-go-round ride once or twice a year, but God forbid that I should have to ride every day of the year and many hours of every day. The social merry-go-round is crowding out everything else in the lives of many of our young people. A young woman said not long ago as naturally as she ever said anything, "Why! there is no time left for the church. It is dinner parties, Saturday evening dances, Sunday afternoon bridge, and the church is crowded out." What a tragic statement for a young woman who has had every advantage wealth could supply!

The greatest thrills come not as we pursue pleasure but as we seek to serve. What's the greatest thrill you have had in the last twelve months? Was it not as you tried to minister to some one in need? Some years ago, while visiting in a small hospital, I heard the screams of a child who cried as if the physician was operating without an anæsthetic. I inquired the cause of the screams. The nurse said, "It is the little boy who was struck by a car. He has not slept in thirty-six hours." I went into his room and found the boy tied hand and foot to his bed and screaming at the top of hisvoice. The nurse was tired and weary. The father and mother came and gave him candy (the worst thing they could have done) and threatened him. So I took charge of

the case. I began to talk to him and as he quieted some-
what he begged that I untie one arm. I said, "On one
condition, and that is that you be quiet and lie here in
bed until the doctor says you can go home." He agreed
and the arm was untied. Immediately he threw it
around my neck and started to pull himself up. But I
reminded him of his promise and he became quiet and
lay back down. Then he begged to have the other arm
untied. This was done on condition that he be a good
boy. Then he begged that one foot be released—the
other leg was broken—and it was untied. Then this
boy with bandaged head and tired body turned about
half over and found an easy position. As I talked with
him, in about three minutes, he was sound asleep—the
first sleep he had had in thirty-six hours. When I left
the hospital I was so thrilled that it was all I could do
to touch the ground. My soul rejoiced, my heart was
filled with supreme happiness. My cup was running
over—because I had been the means of ministering to a
boy whose body had been broken and who needed sleep
above all things else. If you would have a thrill, if you
would find joy that endures, minister to some one in
need, and life will never become dull, gray, nor insipid.

What We Are Here for!

We are here to make a life while we make a living.
Making the life is primary, making the living is secon-
dary. It is rather easy to make a living if one has a
chance at all. It takes very little to live on. The fundamental foods are cheap. But the big thing is making
the life. There are thousands who are making far
more than a living but who are failing utterly in making
a life.

Life is not made by satisfying every whim of the soul, indulging every desire of the body and surfeiting every sense of the flesh. The highest self-expression can only be reached through self-denial. If one would express himself in a lovely home and family, he must deny himself promiscuous living. Every man of influence, position, integrity and power has reached such a pinnacle through self-denial, which always develops a strong, vigorous will power. Most people have too much wishbone and not enough backbone. Too many have become lopsided in their wishing propensities and failed utterly to develop a will power. Some of our wills are as flabby as a day-old pancake and as mushy as a jellyfish. When you strike a hard task, a difficult problem, or a heavy burden, it can't be done or it can be done. If your wishbone is bigger than your backbone, you will say, "It can't be done." But life is not made that way.

Life is made by working out every problem, bearing cheerfully every burden, and being true in every relationship. Hardships may be transformed, and often are, into untold blessings. Life is not one long gala or holiday affair. There are crosses, sorrows, and disappointments. In the natural world there are storms, gales, drouths, and winter blasts. These are sent to develop the fiber of the oaks and elms and by them every root of every tree is sent down deeper into the earth and they bring to perfection the beauty and glory of the mighty giants of the forests.

Some whine and murmur and howl over every hardship; some complain about bearing every cross and despair at every problem. How do you take your hardships and trying experiences? The attitude here will determine and reveal whether you are a cur or a thor-

oughbred.   Ex-president   Theodore   Roosevelt—that
great staunch soul of yesterday—came into his yard one
day and found a cur dog.   He called his boys and said,
"Sons, I want to show you the difference between a cur
and a thoroughbred."   He picked up the cur, slapped
him, pinched him, boxed his ears, twisted his skin and
spanked him.   He howled and yelled and yelped as if
some one were killing him.   When the cur was let go,
he struck for the street and running, yelping, was never
seen again.   Then Mr. Roosevelt picked up the thoroughbred and did him even worse.   There was not a
whimper nor a whine from him.   When he was put
down, the thoroughbred came back ready for another
tussle.   Which are YOU, cur or thoroughbred?   You
can judge yourself.   How do you take your hardships?

Again, life is made by being faithful in the little
things.   As Saul faithfully sought asses, he found a
crown.   As David was faithful in protecting his sheep,
he acquired the skill that brought down Goliath of
Gath. All must begin with little matters, but our fidelity
here means much in the future.

The story is told of two young men, college mates,
who found work in a great garden seed packing plant.
Their work was filling small paper packages with garden seed.   It was wearisome work.   Soon one became
restless and said, "This is no sort of work for me.   I
am quitting."   He quit.   Anybody can quit.   It does
not take brains, brawn, courage, or strength to quit.   He
quit.   But the other young man stayed on.   He did not
work by the clock but by the job.   He was not making
a dollar a day, but was growing a life.   Ten years
came and went.   At the end of ten years the one who
quit was a secretary with a meager salary of $600.00

a year. The other was a high official in the great garden seed business and drawing the handsome salary of $10,000 as an official and big dividends as a stockholder. Life is made as we are faithful in the small tasks and little duties. Prove faithful here and some day, the call, "Come up higher," will sound like sweet music.

Life is made or marred by meeting adequately the crises in life. These crises may come upon us, and often do without a single moment's notice. The call may come out of the blue that will give you the opportunity to stand before princes. The big thing is to be ready when these crises come. The opportunity to make good in a big way does not come often, but we are persuaded it comes. Such times are when one faces the college question, the marriage matter, or some business or spiritual decision. The crossroads in life are critical. What you do then largely mars or makes life.

It is thrilling to hear Dr. George W. Truett tell of his decision for Christ. He was a young schoolteacher, eighteen years of age. A series of meetings in his mountain home church in North Carolina were drawing to a close. A group of young people gathered at a neighbor's home some six miles from the church on a Sunday afternoon "just to be together." The young college student evangelist was with them. As they prepared to return to the church for the evening service, this young preacher said to the young lady friend of the young schoolteacher, "Let me ride with George back to church." She graciously consented. These two young men—one a young schoolteacher, manly, true and faithful; the other a young preacher, faithful and devoted— rode on their horses side by side for six miles. The young preacher brought the young schoolteacher face to face with the greatest issue any man ever faced. All along the way the preacher plead for a decision. The young schoolteacher was facing a crisis. He was at life's critical crossroads. Almost every influence of his home, culture, training, and background was conducive to the right decision, and yet he had not made it. But that evening, in the quiet of his own soul, in the little mountain church, the matchless preacher—that was to be—met the crisis adequately and said, "As man to man, I'll take Jesus as my Saviour." He went forward and as in heaven so on earth, there was great joy. Marvelous events hung on the decision of that young mountain schoolteacher, as he faced a crisis.

Life is found in its fullest when one is true in every relationship. How can the fullest and most complete joy come if we fail anywhere? Who in this world is ever easy with a skeleton in his closet? The one we must all live with is ourself. If we are to have self-respect, we must be true in every relationship. "To live undaunted, unafraid, of any step that I have made." I must measure up in every direction. In East Texas, where many became rich over night with oil, one noble man had, in what became the oil field, a peach orchard. He had agreed with a young man if he would stay on the farm for seven years and tend to this peach orchard he would give him one-fourth interest. All the young tenant had was this man's oral pledge. There was not a sign of a written agreement. The years passed by. The time expired. The young man filled his part of the oral contract. Then he asked for his one-fourth interest. The land now had greatly increased in value. It was in the heart of the world's greatest oil field. Some friends said to the landowner, "He can't collect from you by court. His part is worth now fifty thousand dollars, and all he has is your word." This big man of soul replied, "My word is worth fifty thousand dollars," and he paid him off. How it thrills to know that there are still men in this world whose word is worth fifty thousand dollars! He was true to his word, and if you would find life in its fullest, you, too, must be true and faithful in every relationship.

Life in all its glory is found in doing right. We are to do right, not because it is pleasant or convenient but because it is right to do right. The big word in life is not pleasure, nor riches, but DUTY. Not shunning nor evading nor running from duty, but doing it because of a deep conviction that it is right. Along the pathway that leads to the famous singing tower that Edward Bok erected and equipped in Florida, because of his sheer love of the beautiful, is this inscription on a tablet, "I came here to find myself. It is so easy to get lost in this world."

How true is that of the church! God has set the church along the pathway of life. Its invitation to all is to come in and find yourself—your better and nobler self. It is so easy to get lost in doubt, selfishness, pride, lust, and unbelief. The church is here to help you keep your feet in the path of the righteous that shineth more and more unto the perfect day.

Finally, we are here not to save ourselves but to help save others. As we seek to save others, we will save ourselves. Perhaps you have heard the story of two brothers out in a sleigh on a terribly cold day. They were driving along, wrapped snugly in their fur robes and heavy overcoats. Soon they heard the moans of some poor man in sore need. The one driving reigned up the horses and proposed to investigate. The other objected, saying it was all he could do to keep warm wrapped in the sleigh and he would not expose himself to the raw, bitter cold for any reason, not even to help a dying man.

So the other brother got out and followed the sound of the moans, while one remained wrapped in his furs. Soon the one searching for the source of the groans found a man freezing to death. He pulled, wrestled, tugged, and struggled to arouse this man from his sleep of death. Finally he aroused him and, getting down under him, he got him on his back. As he struggled with his burden and carried the man back to the sleigh, he mopped his brow of the perspiration that stood out like glistening beads. Looking into the sleigh he found his brother cold and stiff in death! Jesus said, "Whosoever shall lose his life for my sake and the gospel's, . . . shall save it." We find life sweet, joyous, and worth while as we invest it for others. Let each one bear witness to the truth by word of mouth, by act of the body, and by the influence of his spirit as Jesus did and life will take on meaning and become purposeful. We are here to serve, and as we serve life will become rich, abundant, and full.

LIVING FOR OTHERS

TEXT: He saved others; himself he cannot save.—Matthew 27: 42.

One of the greatest thoughts ever expressed in a single word came from the lips of a dying man. It is said when General William Boothe, that great old grizzly hero of the cross who had given his life in unselfish service for others, lay dying, he was asked for a message to send around the world. That message from his dying lips was summed up and expressed in one single word—OTHERS. This one word also summed up the career of his great life—the founder of the Salvation Army.

Let us say:

> Lord, help me to live
> From day to day,
> In such a self-forgetful way,
> That even when I kneel to pray
> My prayer shall be for others.

Whenever one discovers that there are others in this world, he has taken a long step toward right living. There are others with rights, others with convictions, others to be taught, others to be trained, others to be healed, others to be reached for Christ.

There are others who are greatly influenced by what we do. There are others whose hearts are broken by our prodigality; others who rejoice in our success and good fortune; others whose heads will hang in shame over our failure; others who are closely and anxiously watching us; others whose very lives will be made or marred by what we do. You are the best Christian some one knows.

This makes life a most serious and solemn responsibility. No man will be satisfied to go to heaven alone. None will ever be content to take this journey by himself. When Andrew found the Lord, he went after his brother. Always there are others who follow us and accompany us. Just so, no man can go to hell alone. The terrible tragedy of sin is that it takes the joy and peace out of more than one life. If our feet were all that were bruised on the rocks of disaster, sin would not be so terrible. But others accompany us on the road of wickedness. Surely, we should think of our loved ones and those who are so near and dear before we venture along the road that leads down.

There are certain boys and girls in every school and community who are leaders in their groups. They lead in the school and in social activity. They lead in play and pastime. They lead in every phase of life and activity except in the highest realm—the religious realm—they forget that there are others waiting, watching, and looking to see what these leaders will do with and for Jesus.

The younger brother many times waits for the older brother. One of the greatest appeals that I know is, "Thy brother is come." You come! Some years ago, two brothers were in business together and had married sisters. They grew up together. They had become a vital part of each other's lives. One night, in a great service in our church, I saw the older one move out from his seat to accept Christ. Then my appeal was, "Thy brother has come. You come." Before the older brother reached the front seat, the younger brother had moved from his seat and started too. Sons are watching fathers, and daughters are waiting for mothers. Godly wives and mothers have influenced whole families for God. What power and mighty influence others have over us!

Leaders ought to lead everywhere. It is the prerogative of leaders to lead. It is their duty and opportunity. In celebrating a victory, Deborah sang, "For that the leaders took the lead in Israel." So many lead everywhere else except in Israel. Leaders should realize that when they fail to lead in the highest realm, they sin grievously against their fellow man. What a joy to see leaders lead spiritually! Some years ago there was in our Sunday school a group of fine football players. They were splendid young men, clean and straight. The captain of the State's Championship Football team was one of that group. He had led his team to victory on the athletic field. We were most anxious to reach them for Christ and bring them to a definite decision. During a service with our Sunday school in mass assembly, these young men, as always, sat together. As the speaker plead for a decision, the captain moved out to take his stand publicly for Christ. Behind him came six other young men—all members of the team—following the fine example he was setting.

Oh! what a power for God and righteousness is a leader who leads in every realm! Pastors ought to lead. They might not give as large gifts as some members of their church, but every pastor can and should lead in

tithing. Deacons and church officials should lead in
Israel. Nothing is more pathetic than deacons who do
not "deak." Sunday school officers and teachers should
lead the way through the gates of glory, "into the
courts of praise."   No group is more responsible for
the six-point record of a pupil being one hundred per
cent than the teachers and officers of a Sunday school.
No man can sell others who has not sold himself.   If
we believe in the virtue of the six-point record system,
let us be ourselves one hundred per cent.   My plea all
down the line and all the way through is that LEADERS
lead.   For their own sake and for the sake of OTHERS,
they should lead.

The devil's plea is to forget others and save yourself.
Come down from the Cross; forget your responsibility;
close your eyes to all social, religious, and domestic
relationships and live for self and self alone.   Cain
forgot that he was his brother's keeper and became the
first murderer.   Esau forgot there were others down
the centuries to be saved and he despised his birthright.
The brothers of Joseph forgot their old father and
themselves and sold their brother into slavery.   Forget
others is the philosophy of the dead-beat, the crook, the
tramp, and the prodigal.   It is the philosophy of sin
and Satan.   Benedict Arnold forgot others in his grasp-
ing greed for money and became America's and the
world's typical traitor.

Let me ask, what are *you* doing—forgetting or re-
membering others?   Are you a weight or wings to
others?   Are you a stumbling-block or a stepping-stone?
Are you closing your eyes to all relationships domestic,
moral, and spiritual?   Or are you assuming the responsibility which God has placed upon you by age,

position, and gift? Every talent and every gift lay on us great responsibility. The women of high estate must reach the lost of high estate. There are two dangerous extremes of society, and both are liabilities. The "ups and outs" and the "downs and outs." I do not know but that the "ups and outs" cause more hell than the "downs and outs." If the ups and outs are ever reached, they must be reached by those who are up in society. If a Christian is blessed with riches, honor, position, and culture, all these add to his responsibility of reaching those about him for Christ. Any highly educated, trained, cultured, competent man, consecrated to Christ, has a further reach in his influence than those not so blessed. Every blessing adds responsibility. Are we assuming it, or evading it?

So many—far too many—accept the philosophy of sin and Satan and forget others. This is tragedy of the most heart-breaking sort. That's the road that Judas traveled, and he went out and hanged himself. That is the path that Benedict Arnold took and died a pauper in a London garret. That is the way that all men take who come to grief and misery and sorrow and wretchedness. The heart and spirit of Christianity are summed up in these words, "Come and receive. Go and tell." Jesus said to his disciples as he called them, "I will make you." What a mighty blessing to others he can make out of any life that is presented to God as a living sacrifice!

Living for others is the law of sacrifice. This law of sacrifice is found in all nature. The candle that saves others from darkness cannot save itself. They tell us that the warm fires that save us from the rigors

of a cold winter are possible only as forests lived and
died ages ago.   Stones used for the building of our
temples of worship, and our homes are solidified frag-
ments of creatures that lived and died millions of years
ago.   Except the grain of wheat fall into the ground
and die, it fails in its full fruition.

The law of sacrifice demands that we give to others
the best we have.   Not SELF-SEEKERS BUT SELF-GIVERS
have lifted the world closer to God.   The foxes have
holes, the birds of the air have nests, but the Son of
man was homeless.   The more like a beast man becomes
—content with material things—the less like Jesus he
is.   The more like Jesus, the more homeless he becomes;
the more like Jesus, the greater spiritual power and
pioneer he becomes.   Christ made himself homeless that
he might prepare a place in his father's house for every
homeless soul.   Jesus said, "I must work the works of
him that sent me while it is day: the night cometh,
when no man can work."   Could not Christ have taken
life easy and reveled in the luxuries of this wonderful
world?   No!   not if he was to work out the plan of salvation and finish it on the cruel Cross for others.   How
busy he was teaching, healing, and blessing everywhere.
He grew tired and weary, but always he was ready to
spend and be spent for others.

His death was for others.   It was an atonement.   He
was the Lamb of God that takes away the sin of the
world.   He became our substitute.   He was made sin
for all men and tasted the bitter dregs of sin's portion
that all men might drink from the cup of salvation.
"He was wounded for our transgressions, he was
bruised for our iniquities: the chastisement of our peace
was upon him; and with his stripes we are healed. . . .

The Lord hath laid on him the iniquity of us all." Did ever any one, anywhere, at any time, do more for suffering, sin-sick humanity than Jesus? Surely, by his death we are reconciled to God and saved from our sins! He became the supreme sacrifice for all ages, filling to the full the prophetic and ceremonial picture of him in the Old Testament.

Blessings always cost. We cannot impart to others without a loss to ourselves. We can never bless fully unless we bleed. Every blessing Jesus bestowed exacted from him time, strength, and energy. When the little timid woman, full of faith, pushed her way through the crowd and touched the hem of his garment and was healed, Jesus said that power went out from him. There's a law in this world as deep as life —if we save ourselves, we cannot save others. The preacher who does not tire himself will tire his audience. The teacher who saves herself and leaves her room as fresh as when she came, has not saved her class from ignorance that day. The business man who does not give himself wholly to his business will soon find that there is no business. If he saves his business, he cannot save himelf. The doctor who saves himself cannot save his patients from disease and illness. If the mother is to save her home from going to pieces, she cannot save herself. So unavoidable is this rigid law that sometime, sooner or later, we all must face and decide whether we will save ourselves or spend and be spent for others.

Influence that endures, widens, blesses, and grips with hoops of steel and lifts to heights sublime, emanates from those who seek to minister to others instead of trying to save themselves. Millions of men today worship Christ, the world is swayed by his mighty influence, not primarily because he is the only begotten Son of God, not because he proved his divine claims by many miracles, but because "the Son of man came not to be ministered unto, but to minister, and to give his life a ransom for many." In the upper room, he did not take a sword as many have; nor a pen, as many others have done; nor a baton, nor a scepter, but a towel, and girding himself he washed his disciples' feet. Buddha said, "I serve no man." Jesus said, "I am a servant to all men."

My heart always thrills over the story of John Maynard, the pilot. He was a pilot on an excursion boat out on one of the Great Lakes. The ship had not sailed many knots when a fire broke out. Its smoke and flame curled up and reached the pilot's house. The captain ordered the passengers to one side and cried to the pilot, "John Maynard." He replied, "Aye, aye." "Head her for the shore," the captain commanded. The pilot turned the boat about and headed her for the shore. The fire grew hotter and the smoke curled and the flame licked like the tongues of demons. One arm of the pilot was limp and hung helpless by his side. What would he do—stay and save the passengers or try to save himself? The captain cried, "John Maynard," and the reply came, "Aye, aye, Sir." "Hold her steady for three minutes." The reply came back, "I will, Sir, God helping me." The heat grew fierce, the smoke was thick, and three minutes seemed to be eternity. But after a while the command came, "John Maynard, beach the ship." With all the force of his mighty engines, he plunged the burning boat on the beach. The passengers were all safely delivered to shore. But days afterwards they picked up John Maynard's body burned badly, floating out on the placid waters. He saved others from tragic death, but he could not save himself.

The law of sacrifice demands volunteer service. Jesus had power to lay down his life and to take it up again. The atoning sacrifice that Jesus made was as willing as if he had nailed himself to the Cross. It was not the nails driven by the soldiers that held him, but the cords of love that bound him. He might have called ten thousand angels to his rescue, but if the Lamb of God was to take away the sin of the world by an atoning sacrifice, he must now to the slaughter be led and submit to the thorns, to the nails, to the spear thrust and to all the ignominy of humanity's foulest spirit. He must endure the enmity of hell without opening his mouth. It was all volunteer from the time he left heaven's court and took upon him the form of flesh, until he ascended on high from Olivet's hill, the cloud receiving him out of sight. Every weary mile of the way he traveled, every precious word he spoke, every blessing he bestowed, and every soul he enlightened, all was done because of his everlasting love for fallen and sin-cursed humanity.

How we should love those who refuse to save themselves, but willingly and lovingly give themselves that we might be blessed!

I shall never forget that day that I stood by my father's bed and watched him, struggling with death, breathe his last. This was my privilege above all the rest of the family. As the last struggle was over, and he grew quiet and still, I took his old hands that were all sunburned, rough, and wrinkled, into mine and leaning over, in deep gratitude, I kissed them and bathed them in tears. Those old sunburned hands, weatherbeaten, had done so much for me! How could I ever repay him? My father came out of the Civil War a penniless young man. He started life in the povertystricken South. He found life's road rudely rough. All that he ever accumulated of this world's riches was done mostly by hard, manual labor. No hired man on his farm ever worked harder than he. Every lick he struck and every day he labored was for one supreme purpose—that his wife and children might find life a bit easier than he found it. Many a time when a barefoot boy, he had picked me up with those old hands and carried me over the rough places to save my tender feet. This was symbolic of all his life. Those dear old hands which are now returning to dust were the sweetest hands that ever I held. He succeeded in saving his family from the rigors of life, but in doing so, he could not save himself. How I love him!

There comes to my mind often a tragic event that I shall never forget. It occurred in my home community when I was a mere lad. A beautiful young mother, with only one child, came into her house after doing some morning chores and saw her precious baby tumble headlong into the fire. She rushed to her screaming baby, picked her up, smothered out the flames and saved her baby from any permanent scars. But the young mother carried to her grave a burned, scarred face, that always had to be dressed and bandaged. That baby has grown to be a woman now, with children of her own. Her mother has gone to be with God. Surely, she never looked on the scarred face of her lov-

ing mother without the tenderest and most affectionate
devotion for her.

I sometimes wonder if we can imagine what Jesus
did for us. We think that this human flesh of ours is
pretty nice. We pamper it, paint it, and powder it.
We think it is an honor to wear it, but you know human
flesh can be the foulest thing on earth. No decomposi-
tion creates a fouler odor than that of a decomposed
human body. Let us try to imagine the only son of a
rich man leaving his beautiful home with all its comforts, with its fellowship, its joy, and pleasures. This
only son turns his back on all that is lovely and beautiful in the ivory palace of his father. Because of his
great love for poverty-stricken people, he lays aside
his suit of broadcloth. He becomes one of a family in
one of these miserable dirt-floor huts. Dressing himself
in the vermin-infested clothes of the poor family, he
lives with them until he has shown them the way of
life. Then imagine, if you can, at his death, which is
tragic, he leaves a will making each one a joint-heir
with him in his father's rich estate. What love and
compassion that would be!

What a poor picture the above is of what Jesus did
for us! He laid aside his royal and shining robes of
glorious light and left heaven's glistening courts where
God's will is done perfectly and his Kingdom's laws
are in the hearts of all the hosts of heaven. He came
into this world of sin and suffering. He dressed himself in the garment of foul flesh that had been defiled
by sin. He wore that garment of flesh, which was always a source of sorrow to him, for thirty-three long
years. Then he willed that whosoever believed in
him and accepted the truth he revealed about his Fa-

ther would be adopted as sons and heirs into his Father's kingdom, sharing with him the unsearchable riches. Then imagine one with such a gracious spirit being taken by men and with cruel hands nailing him to the cross, railing on him and saying, "He saved others, himself he can not save." Surely this was hell condemning heaven; sin sneering at a saviour; error trampling truth in the dust; and Satan trying to overshadow God. Come let us stand right close to the Cross and hear Jesus as he says, in the words of the poet:

> I gave, I gave, My life for thee,
> What hast thou giv'n for Me?
>
> . . . .
>
> I've borne, I've borne it all for thee,
> What hast thou borne for Me?

He saved others; himself he cannot save. If he had saved himself, he could not have saved others. How we ought to love him! Yes!

> Everybody ought to love Jesus,
>
> . . . . . .
>
> He died on the cross to save us from sin,
> Everybody ought to love Jesus.

THE LAND FAIRER THAN DAY

TEXT: . . . To die is gain.—Philippians 1: 21.

Our text is strange language. We never come into the presence of death but that we feel we are in the presence of great mystery. How we would like to lift the veil that separates our dead from us and look into that land we are told is fairer than day! With our limited vision and circumscribed, narrowed experience, we find it exceedingly difficult to believe that to die is gain. But God says it, and we accept it by faith and trust him who does all things well and who knows the other world as he knows this world.

We believe it because the Bible is wonderfully consistent in its teaching, its doctrine, and in its expressions concerning death. It speaks of death as "falling asleep," as a door and entrance into the other world. Jesus said, "Verily, verily, I say unto you, if a man keep my word, he shall never see death." The Jews quoted him as saying, "If a man keep my word, he shall never taste of death." I once thought that these expressions, "never see death" and "never taste of death," were figurative. How could one die and never see death nor taste of death? Surely, it was impossible! Surely, Jesus meant it as a figure of speech! But I am convinced now that Jesus meant these words to be taken literally. Stephen, the first Christian martyr, when he

(184)

died, did not see death. He said, "Behold, I see the heavens opened, and the Son of man standing on the right hand of God." The writer of Acts said, "he, being full of the Holy Spirit, looked up stedfastly into heaven, and saw the glory of God, and Jesus standing on the right hand of God." And when he had prayed, "lay not this sin to their charge," "he fell asleep." Stephen passed through the door of death and experienced death, but he was not conscious nor tasted of it because of what he saw beyond the gates. This so possessed him that he was not conscious of aught else.

The Christian will pass through death and feel the shadow of death, but if we keep the word of Christ, we shall not see it nor taste of it. The sting of death is sin, and for the Christian, Christ has removed the sting. David said, "Though I walk through the valley of the shadow,"—not death, but the valley of the *shadow,*— "of death, I will fear no evil." What evil can harm by casting its shadow upon us? Death, which is the last enemy to be overcome, and an evil which resulted from sin, will cast its shadow, but with Christ, it will not cast its fear. The shadow of a sword has never killed; the shadow of a fire has never burned; the shadow of a serpent has never stung; the shadow of an upias tree has never poisoned, and the shadow of death will never harm. For the one who keeps the Word of Christ, to die is gain, because he will not be conscious nor see this evil as he passes through the gate nor taste of this dreg as the cup is pressed to his lips.

"As a man liveth, so shall he die," has been written or expressed by some one. It is our conviction after more than twenty-five years as a minister that something characteristic of a man's life is found in his death. There are so many illustrations of this that we must believe it is true. There was something horribly fitting in the death of Jezebel, all of whose body was eaten by the dogs in Jezreel except her skull, her feet, and the palms of her hands; in the death of Judas, who hanged himself "and falling headlong, . . . all his bowels gushed out." There seemed to be no compassion in them while he lived; in the death of Absalom, who was caught by the hair of his head as he raised a rebellion against his father. What a tragedy for such a handsome young man! His whole life was one of tragedy.

"Precious in the sight of the Lord is the death of his saints" must mean that God prepares against and arranges for this strange experience of his beloved as he does for all others. "Enoch walked with God: and he was not; for God took him." This quiet, faithful man of God stepped from this world visible into the world invisible; from this world material into the world spiritual. Moses died alone with God on Mount Nebo. Most of his long years he lived alone with God. No man was more lonely than Moses leading Israel through the wilderness. Elijah went up in a whirlwind. Elijah lived in a whirlwind. Wherever he went among men of wickedness, a whirlwind started. Thomas Jefferson and John Adams both died on the fourth of July, and a few hours apart. No two men did more in making that day memorable than these two. Some years ago a noted Texas Baptist preacher died in an automobile wreck. As he had told us something of the story of his great life and ministry, we were impressed that he lived recklessly. When the writer stood by the bedside of his father and watched him die, he struggled hard with death. But his whole life was one long struggle, and he never ceased until he breathed his last. He struggled against poverty and against ignorance. He died in a struggle. Livingstone died on his knees talking to God. We can be sure that he spent much of his time on his knees in prayer to God. In his great mercy, God cares and prepares for the home-going of his people. His grace sufficient for death is given when the time comes. We need never fear that hour nor strange experience if we have lived for him and walked with him.

But why should we ever fear, for God says "to die is gain." The greatest curse that God could pronounce on humanity would be to say that men can never die. If these bodies of ours, so frail, so easily broken, so subject to disease, so apt to be mangled, and so worn and feeble when they begin to give way, could never die, they would prove a burden to man that would crush us beyond words to express.

Some years ago, the writer went with a physician to see a patient who was suffering from a cancer on his jaw. We saw him with his lower jaw tied up with a napkin to keep it from dropping. The ligaments had been eaten away. He was unable to hold his mouth shut. All the nourishment he could take was liquid through a quill because he could not chew. He was suffering intense pain and lying across the bed with his clothes on. He was waiting for death, the only thing that could relieve him. The kind and skilled physician sought only to relieve his acute pain, because there was nothing else to be done nor to be hoped for. He had been told of his hopeless condition and he was waiting—waiting for death to release him from that body that had been damaged beyond repair and the house of clay that was crumbling. As I visited with him and looked on his helpless and hopeless condition, I said in my heart, "Thank God we can die."

If we could not die, if there were no way to move out of this body so weak, so frail, so subject to disease, in one hundred years there would be insane asylums in every town, a hospital in every home, with the crippled and broken bodies of loved ones; we would be so burdened and pressed with the sick, the afflicted, and insane that we could do naught else but care for them. Paul cried, "O wretched man that I am! who shall deliver me from this body of death?" He must have been thinking of that time and occasion when he would lay aside this body as an outworn garment and move into that tabernacle not made with hands! When dust must return to dust, ashes to ashes, and earth to earth! Yes! the greatest curse that God could pronounce would be to say, "Man must live always in this body of clay." Thank God, we can die; that we can move out of this tenement of clay into another world whose land is fairer than day and where we shall never grow old.

The land fairer than day is a place of knowledge. Paul said, in this world we see through a glass darkly, because we know in part and prophesy in part and, like children, we cannot understand all. But then, we shall see face to face and know fully as we are fully known. In that land we shall understand all the deep mysteries of life. All life's riddles will be unraveled and all life's problems will be solved. We will be like Ruth, we shall be satisfied. The word "ruth" means satisfied, and, like Ruth with her lot with God's people, we shall be satisfied. We shall say "Amen" to God's providential dealing with us here. When we trace our pilgrim way and see as God sees, and understand his loving and merciful design in his plans for our lives and in his dealings with us, we shall be satisfied.

> When my spirit, clothed immortal,
> Wings its flight to realms of day,
> This my song thro' endless ages:
> Jesus led me all the way.

That question "Why?" that rises in many souls as they stand beside the new-made grave and watch the form of their loved one, cold and dead, lowered, will be answered in the land fairer than day, and answered to our complete satisfaction. Some years ago, after the writer preached on heaven, a splendid man, a worker in the church and faithful in his devotion and service to God, came and said, "Preacher, you touched on a matter that has baffled me. I have been wholly unable to see *why* God took my wife. We were happy together. Our children had grown to manhood and womanhood. She was a most faithful worker in the church. She loved the Lord and we had sought together to do the will of God and he had blessed us with much and with many of his mercies. Then death came and broke up our happy home and left it a desolate, lonesome place. Preacher, I can't understand *why!*" I heard his heart-breaking story of sorrow and I said, "Some day, some day, my brother, in that land, God will answer that question that has baffled you through the years." Yes! some day, every question of every heart that understands only in part now, will be answered and we shall know why and say "Amen."

Again, it is a land of supreme joy. In every heart, joy will reign supreme. In this world of semi-circled rainbows; in this world where there "are always clouds that gather after the rain and where hearts may rejoice at one hour and be broken with grief at another, we never know the fulness of joy." But yonder where "all things will be made new," where there will be "no disagreeable memories, no devastated homes, no dispossession, no disappointed hopes, no decay and death," we shall know the fulness of the joy of our Lord.

Jesus tried to tell us about it. He said it would be as a shepherd who went out and found his sheep that was lost and bringing it in on his shoulders, he would call together his friends and neighbors and say, "Rejoice with me; for I have found my sheep which was lost." Jesus said, "Even so," . . . just like that,—"joy shall be in heaven over one sinner that repenteth." The greatest joy that heaven knows is when a man on his road to hell turns toward God and cries in his soul, "God be merciful to me a sinner." When the Seventy returned to Jesus and told him of their glorious success, he said, "I beheld Satan fallen as lightning from heaven" and it is said, "In that same hour he rejoiced in the Holy Spirit." In the words of another, "When we join that white-robed, blood-washed throng, the supreme note of our souls will be joy." The joy of the shepherd who found his lost sheep, of the woman who found her lost coin, and of the father who welcomes his lost son back home, will be ours.

Then, too, the land will be a place of holy fellowship. Christ's last and greatest commission was, "Make disciples of all nations," for they shall come from the east and from the west and sit down with Abraham,

Isaac, and Jacob in his Kingdom. What holy fellowship will be ours with the great and good and the noble from every point of the compass as they gather in the city of God! John said he saw the gates—twelve of them in all—an abundant entrance. On the east were three gates; on the north were three gates; on the west, three gates, and on the south, three gates.

There will be sweet fellowship with our own loved ones who have gone on before. We do not lose those who die. We are only separated from them. They are as much ours as those who remain here. Some years ago the writer heard a Negro spiritual which expressed it:

> I have a father, over in Zion,
> And he's mine, he's mine, he's mine.
> I have a mother over in Zion,
> And she's mine, she's mine, she's mine.
> I have a baby over in Zion,
> And it's mine, it's mine, it's mine.

This great truth is taught specifically in the Word. Jacob, after his long and winding pilgrimage, said, "I am to be gathered unto my people." We say, "separated," but God says "gathered." Jacob had many of his loved ones in that fair land. Look in the story of Job. As he lost all that he prized most dearly,—his sheep, his camels, his asses, his servants, and, finally, his ten children at one stroke,—what a blow was his! When his wealth had vanished and his family had been struck down at one great blow, his health gave way. His wife broke with him and advised him to give up his faith in God. But the strong man of God, in his poverty and wretched health, cried, 'Though he slay me. yet will I trust him." And trust him he did. Then there came a change in his fortune. God added to him twice as much at the latter end as he had in the beginning. God doubled his sheep; doubled his camels; doubled his oxen, and doubled his she-asses, but gave him only ten children! Why doesn't it say that he had twenty children given him? We would say that he lost his first ten. But those of his children on the other side were just as much Job's as the ten on this side of the river. When God gave him ten more, then his children were doubled, too. No! those over yonder, beyond the river, are just as much our loved ones as those over here. What blessed fellowship, what glorious experiences will be ours when the family circle that has been broken shall be made whole again never to be severed! Heaven's blessing of fellowship is a joy that shall be ours in its fulness.

This holy fellowship demands that the land fairer than day be a place where we shall know one another. We shall know one another better when the mists have rolled away. When we rise above this mirky, foggy atmosphere of earth, we shall know as we are fully known. One question that many have often asked about their departed loved ones is, "Shall we know them in heaven?" God satisfies no longing of the human heart more definitely than he does this yearning. He says, "There is one glory of the sun, another glory of the moon, and another glory of the stars; for one star differeth from another star in glory. So also"—just like that—"is the resurrection of the dead."

Science tells us that no two leaves of the billions on billions are exactly alike; no two blades of grass are alike, and no two stars are alike in their glory. If God can give to every blade of grass, every leaf on the many trees, and every star of the billions twinkling in the vaulted heavens, their glory, then he is abundantly able to give to every soul its personality in the resurrection of the dead. Peter, James, and John recognized Moses and Elijah as they talked with Jesus about his death on the Mount of Transfiguration. The disciples recognized instantly Jesus when he appeared in his resurrection glory. Yonder on the shore of blue Galilee when he asked them in the early morning if they had aught to eat, the disciple, whom Jesus loved, said to impetuous Peter, "It is the Lord." And Peter plunged into the sea and was drawn to him like a magnet.

He was the same Christ that walked on the billowy waves and came to them one stormy night. He was the same Christ that spoke to the angry winds and stormy sea, saying, "Peace, be still." He was the same Christ that spoke to the "legion" in the demoniac, and they came out of the man. He was the same Christ who spoke to the little daughter of Jairus, and she arose and walked; the same Christ that spoke to the widow's son of Nain as he was being carried to the city of the dead, and he sat up and was given back to his weeping mother. He was the same Christ that spoke to his friend, Lazarus, who had been dead three days and was in his grave and he came forth. Yes! the same Christ who took the three loaves and five fishes and fed the hungry multitude. No question of the human heart is answered more definitely than that we shall know our loved ones when the mists have cleared away.

Another question that puzzles many and brings grief to troubled souls who do not consult God's Word but frequent the places of quackery and fraud is, "What becomes of the soul when the body dies?" God's Word states unmistakably that there are two places for a saved soul—present in the body and absent from the Lord, or absent from the body and at home with the Lord. Paul was torn between two desires, whether to be absent from the body and present with the Lord or at home in the body and absent from the Lord. David said of his beloved child, "I shall go to him, but he shall not return to me." Jesus said to the penitent, dying thief, who cried, "Lord, remember me when thou comest into thy kingdom," "Verily I say unto thee, Today shalt thou be with me in paradise." Some would place the little comma here after "today" and build on that little comma a whole false theory of the dead. All the Word of God demands that the comma be placed after "thee." It was that day that he died, that day that he paid sin's debt on the Cross, that day he redeemed the dying thief that he was to be with Jesus in Paradise. We would save ourselves great grief and sore anxiety if we would take the plain, simple Word of God and accept it and rest on it for the great doctrine of the future life.

Yes! death is a blessing in disguise. To die is truly and really gain. It affords a marvelous opportunity to witness for Christ when we approach it with our faith in God and our hope placed in him. Paul said it was his earnest expectation and hope to magnify Christ in his body whether by life or by death. If by life he could better magnify Christ he would live, for "For me to live is Christ," but if by death he could better magnify Christ, he would die, for "to die is gain."

It was by death that Samson, the mighty man of strength, slew many of the Philistines. You know the story of how, when poor old Samson, blind and led by a lad, was brought to the temple of Dagon "to make sport" for those whose "hearts were merry," he was set between the pillars. He said to the lad that held him by the hand, "Suffer me that I may feel the pillars whereupon the house standeth that I may lean upon them." He made sport for the last time to the house full of men and women and crowded upon the roof. Poor old blind Samson prayed a pitiful prayer, saying: "O Lord Jehovah, remember me, I pray thee, and strengthen me, I pray thee, only this once. O God, that I may be at once avenged of the Philistines for my two eyes." And feeling his old strength surge back through his bent form, he cried, "Let me die with the Philistines," and bowing himself, the pillars were pulled and the house of merriment was turned into a house of death and carnage. He slew more at his death than he slew in his life.

I am praying that God might give me the opportunity to witness and bear testimony for my Lord when I come to die. Yes! I would like to take his Cross at my death and strike the devil a final blow as I passed into the land fairer than day. Some preach their greatest sermon in their death. When America entered the World War, a friend had an orphan boy who had been taken into his home and made one with his fine little family. His name was Ben Odam, a quiet, modest boy, who was a sincere Christian. Ben was drafted, and the time came to leave his adopted home. Loving Ben as a son, my friend, Dr. J. D. Crain took him into his study and reading some scriptures, said, "Ben, do you believe that?" "Yes," he replied, "I believe it." And reading some more from the Word, he said, "Do you believe that?" "Yes, I am resting my soul on that." Then he said, "Ben, my boy, if you must go, go and magnify

Christ; and if you never come back, magnify him in death."

Ben left home and the homeland with a heavy heart. He served in France, and while serving as a faithful soldier, trouble developed in his ears. Over there, he was sent to a hospital and while being treated in the army hospital, the armistice was signed. Then the soldiers began to return home and the doctors told Ben if he would stay with them, they could cure him, but if he insisted on taking his place as his turn came to go back, they would not prevent his going. Ben was homesick and insisted on taking his place in his turn on the transport, for he was much better.

So while the great transport, crowded with returning soldiers, was on the high seas, Ben was placed on guard duty. While on guard duty, his old trouble returned. He called for the corporal of the guard and told him that he was sick and wished to be relieved. Thinking that Ben was trying to evade duty, he replied, "Boy, you are not sick. Stay on." But Ben was sick and grew worse and finally was carried to the infirmary. That night as he grew rapidly worse, my friend said, "Jesus walked on the water again, and coming to this quiet, faithful soul, said, 'Ben, thou shalt not sink,' and lifed him out of his body of clay." And Ben went to be at home with his Lord.

They took Ben's body, wrapped it in tow, put weights on his feet and laid it out over the deck of the great ship and covered it with "Old Glory." The soldiers on board, stood with bowed, uncovered heads as a chaplain said some words and committed the body to a watery grave. Then the plank on which the body was lying was tilted and the body of Ben Odam dropped to

the bottom of the sea. It is said that so impressive was
this burial of the modest lad at sea, no man on board
spoke that evening above a whisper. God spoke to their
hearts in the still small voice more effectively than he
had in the belching of smoke and fire on Flanders fields.
In his death and burial, this quiet, modest lad magnified
his Lord and preached a sermon that reached the hearts
of the thousands returning home.

What an abundant entrance will be ours as the gates
swing open and the Redeemer receives and welcomes
those saved by grace! From another come the thoughts,
"We are too stupid about death." We will not learn
how it is wages paid and the gift for which we all
yearn. It is winning heaven's eternal gain and free-
dom from earth's pain. We count our griefs more than
we consider their relief. We think of the separation and
forget the gathering where bright angels' feet have
trod.

What great joy will be the weary pilgrim's, the heroic
soldier's, and the faithful servant's as Christ awaits and
welcomes them! Yonder in Furman University, the
writer's alma mater, was a teacher, one of the finest of
laymen, Professor Lueco Gunter. Never having married, his sister made her home with him and made a
home for him. In the course of the years there developed trouble in his spinal column. After seeking
relief from skilled specialists in many places, and
thinking that the cause had been located and removed,
he returned to his home to recuperate. But soon, the old
trouble came back worse than ever. Rapidly he became
seriously ill and the day came when the Master was to
call his faithful servant. When the hour was upon him,
he looked up at his sister by his side and with a frown,

he asked, "Where is Jesus?" and his sister, bending over him, said, "He is right here." Then he cried, "Will Jesus go with me?" "Yes," she said, "Jesus will go with you, my dear." A smile played over his face as he breathed his last and said, "Blessed Jesus, blessed Jesus." I would rather have that sweet experience with my Master as I pass through the gates than all the gold and silver piled mountain high. I would rather have that joy than all the fleeting pleasures this world can give. I would rather have that warm welcome than all the honors that man could heap upon me.

The land fairer than day might not be so very far away. A few more years, a few more days! Ah! a few more hours! and the servant might knock at our door and call us to come! Dr. J. W. Chapman used to tell the story of a man who came hurriedly one morning to his study and, weeping like his heart would break, he said, "Come, doctor, quick, mother is gone!" Then he sat down and after weeping, told how, the night before, his mother joined with them in their family worship; how she took her little oil lamp and as she passed through the door up to her room, she turned and, holding the lamp up, her face beaming with joy, she said, "Goodnight, I'll see you in the morning." He said, "She never looked better than when she bade us goodnight." Then he continued, "This morning, we waited and she didn't come. Then we went to her room and knocked gently, but there was no answer. Finally, we went in and found her body cold and stiff in death." Then the strong man broke down again and wept bitterly and said, "No! it won't be long. We'll see her in the morning. We'll see her in the morning."

It won't be long, may not be as long as we think!

One sweetly, solemn thought
    Comes to me o'er and o'er;
I'm nearer home today
    Than I have been before.

Nearer my father's house,
    Where the many mansions be;
Nearer the great white throne today,
    Nearer the crystal sea.

Nearer the bound of life,
    Where burdens are laid down;
Nearer to leave the cross today,
    And nearer to the crown.

Be near when my feet
    Are slipping o'er the brink;
For I am nearer home today,
    Perhaps, than now I think!

And what a marvelous invitation God has extended to every lost soul to come! When the Book, God's message to man, was to be closed, the pen was in the hand of John on Patmos. It has been said that as the beloved disciple wrote, God whispered, "John, I want you to extend to the lost world my final invitation that every soul may know I want him to come!" And John took up his pen and wrote, "The Spirit and the bride say, Come"—and laid his pen down. Then God said, "John, that is hardly strong enough, the world must echo this invitation." And John took up his pen and wrote, "And let him that heareth say, Come"—and laid his pen down again. Then God said, "John, somebody might not understand. Can't you make it more general?" And John took his pen again and wrote, "And let him that is athirst come"—and laid it aside. Then God whispered, "John, won't you try one more time? Somebody might not understand. Can't you make it more universal?" And John took his pen again and wrote, "And whosoever will, let him take the water of life freely." Did man ever write, read, or receive a more general, universal, worldwide invitation anywhere than that which God placed at the close of his Book? Oh! dear friend, if you fail to come, if you fail to respond, if you miss this fair and happy land, with its streets of gold and gates of pearl, it will not be because of God's failure to invite you, but because of your unwillingness to believe and accept. "Whosoever will" means me, means you, and every lost soul anywhere in this wide, wide world.